D0245723

MARITIME BRITAIN

RICHARD HILL

'...your seamen are the life of your fleet; and your fleet is the security and protection of your trade; and both together are the wealth, strength, security and glory of Britain'.

P

Publication in this form copyright © Jarrold Publishing 2005.
Text copyright © Jarrold Publishing.
The moral right of the author has been asserted.
Series editor Angela Royston.
Edited by John McIlwain.
Designed by Nick Avery.
Cover designed by Simon Borrough.
Picture research by Christine Crawshaw.

The photographs are reproduced by kind permission of:
The Advertising Archive 70l; Peter Aprahamian 78; The Art Archive 42t (British Library), 45tr (Bibliothèque des Arts Décoratifs Paris/Dagli Orti), 48–49 (Biblioteca Nacional Madrid/Dagli Orti), 83b (Ocean Memorabilia Collection); Author's Collection 58t, 79b; By kind permission of His Grace the Duke of Bedford and the Trustees of the Bedford Estates 24b; Bibliothèque nationale de France 8; Bluegreen 75l (Rick Tomlinson); The Bodleian Library, University of Oxford 16t (MS.Douce.208.f.120v); www.bridgeman.co.uk fc main (Royal Naval Museum, Portsmouth), 9t (Winchester Corporation, Hampshire), 9b, 13, 22b & 45tl (British Library), 10 (Museo Torlonia, Rome/Alinari), 12l (Viking Ship Museum, Oslo, Norway), bc, 12r, 27t & 37b (British Museum), 20–21 (Musée de la Marine, Paris), 24t (Kunsthistoriches Museum, Vienna), 39t (Private Collection/Phillips, The International Fine Art Auctioneers), 41b & 62b (The Stapleton Collection), 47 (Fitzwilliam Museum, University of Cambridge), 55t (Bonhams, London); © BP plc. 2004 93t; www.britainonview.com 75b; British Library 11b, 15c, 17, 28t, 29, 31b; © The British Museum/Heritage-Images 39b; © David Cobb 5; Corbis 7 (© Sean Sexton collection); Crown Copyright, image from www.photos.mod.uk, reproduced with the permission of the Controller of Her Majesty's Stationery Office 89b (photograph by POA (Phot) Paul Smith), 90t (photograph by Neptune Phot Section), 90b (photograph by LA (Phot) Gary Davies); Cunard Image Library 94b; English Heritage Photo Library 4 (Graeme Peacock), 11t (Jonathan Bailey), 18 (Nigel Corrie), 69b (G P Darwin on behalf of Darwin Heirlooms Trust/photo Jonathan Bailey); Mary Evans Picture Library 44, 51bl, 61b, 70–71, 74, 76; Getty Images 66b, 80r, 82b; SS Great Britain Trust 60; Robert Harding Picture Library 56l; Michael Holford fc tc, 6, 14,15t, 15b, 48b; The Illustrated London News Picture Library 68; Imperial War Museum 86 (LD305), 87b (B5218), 88tl (Q20640), 88–89 (FKD 2387/private copyright), 91t (FKD2610); Jarrold Publishing 36, 71r; Maritime Museum, Rotterdam 16b; The Mary Rose Trust 21b, 23b; By kind permission of the Masters of the Bench of the Honourable Society of the Middle Temple 25; © National Gallery, London 63; National Maritime Museum 19t, 19b, 26t, 26–27, 30, 31t, 32, 33t, 33b, 34–35, 35b, 37t, 38, 40t, 40b, 42–43, 43t, 46l, 46r, 49r, 50, 51t, 51br, 53t, 53b, 55bl, 55br, 62t, 64–65, 66t, 67, 69tl, 72b, 77t, 77b, 79t, 80l, 81b, 83tr, 87t; National Portrait Gallery 20tl, 28b, 34b, 45b, 64l; The Natural History Museum, London 69tr; Peter Newark's Pictures 52; Robert Opie 61t; Pepys Library, Magdalene College, Cambridge 20b, 22–23; Pictures of Britain 73t; P&O Nedlloyd 92; P&O Ferries 93b; Popperfoto 81t; By kind permission of the RMS Queen Mary Foundation 82–83 (from Art of the RMS Queen Mary by Douglas M Hinkey, catalogue of exhibition originally at Hippodrome Gallery); Rex Features 73b, 91b; Royal Geographical Society fc background; Royal Naval Museum, Portsmouth 58b, 59; Skyscan Photolibrary 54; The Sutcliffe Gallery 72t; Topham Picturepoint 94t; Trinity House 75tr; By kind permission of the Warrior Preservation Trust 65t; Wellcome Library, London 41t.

The artwork was created by Roger Hutchins. The drawing of HMS Victory on pages 56–57 is reproduced by kind permission of Living History magazine.

The map on the inside front cover was created by The Map Studio Ltd, Romsey, Hampshire.

The extract from Cargoes on page 70 is published by kind permission of The Society of Authors, Literary Representatives of the Estate of John Masefield.

All rights reserved. No part of this publication may be reproduced, stored in a retrieval system or transmitted in any form or by any means (electronic, mechanical, photocopying, recording or otherwise) without the prior written permission of the publisher and the copyright holders.

A CIP catalogue for this book is available from the British Library.

Published by:
Jarrold Publishing
Healey House, Dene Road, Andover, Hampshire,
SP10 2AA
www.britguides.com

Set in Minion.
Printed in Singapore.

ISBN 1 84165 128 1   1/05

 Pitkin is an imprint of Jarrold Publishing, Norwich.

CONTENTS

BRITAIN'S NAUTICAL HERITAGE

SAIL BEATS STEAM

David Cobb's fine painting recalls the incident in 1888 when the veteran clipper Cutty Sark, *outward bound for Australia, overhauled the mail steamer* Britannia, *arriving in Sydney several hours ahead of her newly-built rival.* Cutty Sark *is now preserved at Greenwich, London.*

FOR 15,000 YEARS, SINCE the Ice Age receded and the sea rushed in to leave Britain as a group of islands, the only way of getting there was by sea. The first settlers, Stone Age hunters, walked over land bridges from mainland Europe; later arrivals, until 20th-century developments brought new means of connection with the wider world, had to come and go by ship.

Maritime Britain's history has been made by people who lived from and with the sea. The sea gave people around the coasts a livelihood, as fishermen and traders, seafarers and shipbuilders, smugglers and pirates. The sea offered invaders a route in, and explorers a way out. The sea was not only Britain's

defence, but also an avenue for adventure, and expansion. As Britain evolved into a colonial and imperial power, few of its rulers could afford to turn their gaze from the sea for long.

To a great extent, our island geography still rules. Well over 90 per cent of imported goods, by volume, still come into Britain by sea. Ports remain important economic assets, as they have been since Roman ships sailed up the Thames to London. The City of London's maritime-related institutions, internationally respected, still add greatly to the national wealth, as do maritime industries such as electronics, charting, weapons and cargo handling. The Royal Navy, though much diminished, is still

LOOK TO THE SEA

The estuary of the River Aln, Northumberland, where it meets the North Sea.

5

'Your Fleet and your Trade have so near a relation and such mutual influence on each other, they cannot well be separated; your trade is the mother and nurse of your seamen; your seamen are the life of your fleet; and your fleet is the security and protection of your trade; and both together are the wealth, strength, security and glory of Britain.'

A contemporary view of British sea power nearing its height: Lord Haversham (1647–1710)

THE MARINER'S COMPASS

A wooden bowl for a magnetic compass, made by William Farmer in about 1750.

among the most powerful in the world. Shipbuilding has declined, as have fisheries, though the latter remain a valuable resource – if properly managed. In addition, offshore oil and gas have been harnessed since the 1970s.

⸺

Britain's maritime heritage attracts millions of visitors to dockyards, historic ships and naval museums, and most people still know at least the names of the nation's greatest maritime heroes – Drake, Cook and Nelson. The seaside retains its appeal to many holidaymakers, despite the counter-attractions of package flights to beaches far away; weekend sailing, surfboarding, water sports and diving attract a new generation of enthusiasts. While in comparison with a century ago the sea commands less attention, even a people now living predominantly in cities can still thrill to tales and images of the sea and ships. As a Second World War minesweeper skipper observed: almost any Briton can make a seaman in a month or so – once he (or she) has got over the seasickness.

⸺

After victory in the Napoleonic Wars in 1815 (a victory won at Waterloo but ensured by Trafalgar ten years before), Britain's dominant position for the rest of the 19th century rested firmly on superiority at sea. Britain's trade was oceanic; its demand for raw materials and 'free trade' was backed by the world's biggest and, from the 1860s, most technically advanced navy. The Royal Navy's battleships were the power base for Pax Britannica and its cruisers patrolled the sea routes between mother country and empire.

⸺

The Victorian age marked the peak of Britain's power. By the 1900s, power was shifting. After the carnage of the First World War, in which the Navy played a supportive role and the submarine emerged as the most deadly threat to its ocean lifelines, Britain's maritime and industrial might decayed. Trade suffered from recession, the Navy from lack of resources. Even so, in the Second World War Britain fought a successful maritime campaign, not least due to the tenacity and training of her seamen. In the uneasy decades of the Cold War and the turbulent peace that followed, with Britain now a medium world power, giving up an empire and seeking a new role, maritime confidence and enterprise again tended to ebb away. The global economy shifted traditional industries (such as shipbuilding) away from Britain, but the Navy remained

capable of holding the stage, as it did during the Falklands campaign of 1982.

∽

Britain's nautical past makes a great story and, as sea artists have always known and proved, lends itself to stunning illustration. The reader who enjoys the summary in these pages may want to set course into other waters, exploring more aspects of maritime history and literature, through the numerous museum and maritime sites around the country. Some readers too may find pointers to a more prosperous maritime future. Whatever course they choose, the author wishes them a good voyage.

SEAFARERS

The traditional face of British maritime life and, many believe, its essential core: hardy, humorous and bred to the sea.

'Keep then the sea that is the Wall of England
And then is England kept by Goddes own hand.'

The Libelle of Englyshe Policie, c.1436

INVADERS

THE FIRST INHABITANTS OF Britain were Stone-Age hunter-gatherers, hill and woodland dwellers who were generally fearful of the ocean – although they did, out of necessity, use rivers and lakes for fishing and transport.

Around 5000 BC, as the last Ice Age ended, melting ice sheets caused sea levels to rise and Britain became an island. Soon waves of seaborne incomers began to arrive. These folk, besides building boats, were resourceful farmers and manufacturers. The Beaker people, about 4,000 years ago, introduced bronze culture. The Celts, a thousand years later, brought the Iron Age, fine art, horses and chariots. Water transport, inland and coastal, played a significant part in this developing civilization.

In AD 43, the Romans came in force to settle. Brilliantly organized, they won over some British tribes and subdued others, using the sea to supply their legions and for trade with their empire.

When they departed after 400 years of occupation, Britain was exposed to new raiders. Seafaring fighters and farmers from across the North Sea – Saxons, Angles and Jutes – came in ships, seized the most fertile land and pushed the Celtic-Roman British further west. Saxon 'England', a medley of kingdoms, was from the 800s itself menaced by Viking sea-raiders, and finally overthrown by a seaborne invasion, the Norman Conquest of 1066.

For the next four centuries, England (with substantial French royal lands) and Scotland (with close ties to Scandinavia) learned more fully how to use the sea. Ships were built for trade, for defence, for military expeditions and for fishing. Few of them ventured south beyond the Bay of Biscay, or east and north beyond the great ports of Hanseatic Germany. But the people of the British Isles were becoming ever more conscious of the value of the sea to their prosperity and independence.

THE WINCHELSEA SEAL
The ancient seal of this former East Sussex port shows all the essentials of a medieval ship: mast, sail, steering oar, fore and after 'castles'.

BATTLE BY SEA
Before the age of guns, fighting was at close quarters and throwing overboard was a favoured way of disposing of the enemy.

SPREADING THE WORD
Thomas Becket landing at Sandwich, Kent, in disregard of royal warnings.

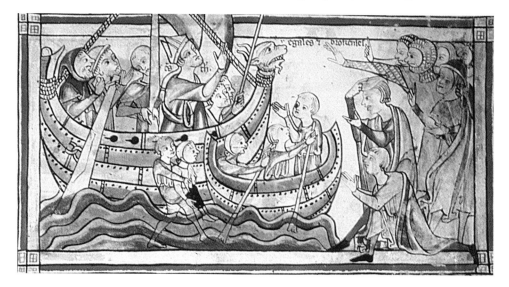

THE LEGIONS AND THE GOSPEL

JULIUS CAESAR FIRST CAME to Britain in 55 BC. In his subsequent account, he wrote of his expedition as a raid or at most a reconnaissance in force. That put the best possible gloss on it. The infantry got ashore at Walmer in Kent, but the cavalry did not, owing to storms and tides. The landing could not be sustained and in the autumn Caesar retired to Gaul.

Over the winter, Rome's most ambitious general built a new fleet of warships and transports. The new ships were better suited to Channel conditions; all of them were fitted with sails, though oars were still used for motive power and when manoeuvring. Caesar's expedition of 54 BC consisted of 800 ships with 30,000 men, and this time the horse transports landed their charges successfully in the area of Sandwich.

As in the previous year, storms wrecked much of the invasion fleet on the beach.

Guerrilla attacks by the British tribes proved equally violent. Nevertheless, Caesar succeeded in marching his legions north, beyond where London now stands, before withdrawing from the island in good order in September.

Although there was no further landing over the next hundred years, Roman interest in Britain continued. Cross-Channel trade flourished, but non-Roman Britain posed a security threat to Roman Gaul. Accordingly, Rome's emperor Claudius, needing a triumph to boost his popularity at home, decreed that the southern part of Britain should be occupied, and in AD 43 legions from the Rhine area, under the command of Aulus Plautius, made unopposed landings on the Kent coast, near what is now Richborough.

The invaders faced stiff opposition in the north and north-east, but subdued it

'Jump, comrades, unless you wish to betray our eagle to the enemy; I, at any rate, intend to do my duty to our country and my commander.'

Standard bearer of the X Legion, landing in 55 BC

A FORT OF THE SAXON SHORE

Portchester Castle in Hampshire still stands as a monument of Roman fortification against Saxon raids.

with a mixture of brute force, pacification and bribery. Making London their capital, the Romans soon won over the southern British to the good life of Roman mercantilism and by AD 60 London and several Channel ports had become flourishing centres of commerce. Roman technical skills were also harnessed at river wharves, the underwater lines of cargo vessels being modified so that they settled safely on the mud as the tide fell. The sea played a vital part in Roman control. Not only was it a channel for exports of wool, grain and tin, and imports of wine and manufactures, but its military potential was exploited. Fleets supported the Roman army on expeditions in the north and also conducted patrols against North Sea pirates, held at bay by the stone forts of the 'Saxon Shore'.

As the Roman Empire came under increasing pressure along its far-stretched frontiers, this control ebbed away. In the early 400s, the legions departed, leaving towns and fortresses to decay. The Saxons, some of whom were hired by the Roman-British as mercenaries, moved in

without naval challenge. The so-called Dark Ages began, but the sea still played a vital part, not only in trade, but in the traffic of ideas. Celtic missionaries in small boats crossed the sea to spread the Christian faith in the north, while across the Channel came St Augustine to convert the south. These voyages were often made in craft that would today seem absurdly small, little more than coracles. Yet the sea provided a highway, when so much of the land was wilderness and war-torn. In the centuries to come, Britain's peoples might still look on the sea with fear and wonder: they would never ignore it.

THE SAINTS COME ROWING IN

Although the scale may be exaggerated, Christian missionaries did come from Ireland and Scotland in tiny craft.

11

DRAGONS FROM THE SEA

THE PROW

Detail of the prow of the Viking longship excavated at Gokstad, Norway, now in the Viking Ship Museum at Oslo.

THE FIRST SIGHT of the Norse invaders deserved its dramatic description. The Vikings' sudden appearance from the open sea, or slipping up river estuaries, struck panic into the English, Welsh and Scots who suffered at their hands. Viking longships were seaworthy enough to sail from Scandinavia: of shallow draught and powered principally by oars, they carried a single square sail for use in favourable winds. The warriors who manned them were formidable fighters, armed with sword, spear and axe.

The English, by now less accustomed to seafaring than their Saxon forebears, resisted the Vikings with varying success. England was divided into several kingdoms, and there was no semblance of national unity until a king of Wessex emerged who turned out to be a match for the invaders.

Alfred the Great (849–99) was chiefly a battlefield commander, and for much of his reign relied on mobile land forces linked by well-fortified coastal defences. But in the last few years of his reign Alfred built a large and novel sea-fighting force, and for this he is entitled to be called

MENACE AND PROTECTION

A Saxon warrior's helmet, perhaps once belonging to King Raedwald of the East Angles, from a buried ship discovered at Sutton Hoo, Suffolk.

the 'father of the English Navy'. The English ships were probably bigger than their Viking counterparts, stouter and higher out of the water, so making them better all-round craft in Channel conditions. Battles were seldom fought at sea; skirmishes tended to take place on the coast or river bank, between warriors from ships that were by then at anchor or

'Terrible portents appeared over Northumbria … fiery dragons were seen flying in the air … rapine and slaughter.'

The Anglo-Saxon Chronicle, 793

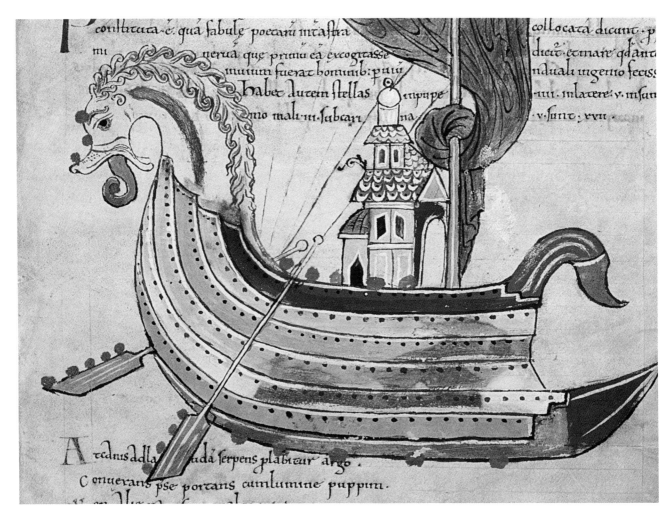

constituta e. qua fabule poetarii mastra
mi   nerua que primu ea excogitasse
*   mutum fuerat hominibus: prui*
*   habet lucem stellas*
mo mali m. subcari   na

collocata dicant .p
dicit ecinaie qdant
nduali ingenio fecis
mi . mlatere : v. msun
v. sunt : xvn ·

A tednus adla   uda serpens plabicur argo .
Conuerans pse porcans cumlumine puppim .

DRAGON SHIP

From a 10th-century manuscript, this picture clearly shows the overlapping (clinker) construction of the hull.

even aground. Alfred's fleet was intended as a deterrent, able if necessary to close with the enemy at sea to prevent them from landing.

In the 10th century, after further successes by Alfred's immediate descendants, English sea power was allowed to wither and Danish Vikings re-established their dominance, so much so that in the early 1000s England had a Danish king, Cnut, who ruled a North Sea empire (England, Norway and Denmark). On his death in 1035, the dynasties became confused, rivalries festered, and opportunists waited their chance. William of Normandy, bred from Viking stock, saw his chance in 1066.

THE VIKING IMPACT

The Vikings were efficient in plunder, often with great violence, and in extortion of money in return for being left alone. They were also remarkable traders, ranging as far afield as Russia and Constantinople. They made Dublin and York (Jorvik) into thriving centres of trade. Viking families also settled to farm, mainly in east and north-east England, Scotland and the Orkneys, leaving a permanent legacy in language and place names.

HIC WILLELM DUX IUSSIT NAVES EDIFICARE

RAMCIS

ORDERS FOR CONQUEST

In the Bayeux Tapestry, Duke William of Normandy orders the felling of timber, part of the huge effort necessary to build an invasion fleet.

HISTORY SHOULD HAVE TAUGHT any English king to look seaward for potential enemies (as well as at his family and court). After Edward the Confessor died in January 1066, Harold Godwinson was chosen as king but his accession to the throne was at once challenged by two other claimants: Harald Hardrada of Norway and Duke William of Normandy.

William claimed Edward had promised him the crown, and accused Harold of reneging on an earlier oath of loyalty. He began assembling and manning an invasion fleet. Harold watched the south coast, but faced a more imminent threat in the north, where his brother Tostig, in league with Harald Hardrada, appeared with a ship-borne Norwegian army in the summer of 1066.

Harold possessed a powerful fleet. He could have barred William's crossing, but time was not on his side. As soon as the Norwegians landed east of York, Harold marched his army north to meet them. On 25 September he comprehensively defeated Hardrada and Tostig at Stamford Bridge on the River Ouse, with the help of some English ships that had retreated up-river before the invaders.

This rapid and complete victory could not secure Harold's future, for three days later William crossed the Channel with the force he had been building up all the summer. At least 700 vessels, built on the Viking-English pattern with both oars and sails, carried his army and its horses. They were vulnerable to attack both at sea and on the landing beaches.

Good planning on the Norman side, for which there is plenty of evidence, was backed, therefore, by luck. The Norwegian attack in the north had drawn off Harold's land force at a critical time. Crucially, the English navy, having been on the watch for William's invasion all summer, had withdrawn to replenish with supplies – by some accounts, as far away as London.

So when Duke William set foot on the beach at Pevensey on 28 September, he had crossed the Channel unopposed.

> ‘Who could hope … that the Norman ships would be ready in time, or that suffi-cient oarsmen would be found within a year?’
>
> *William of Poitiers, c.1070*

BUILDING THE FLEET
Shipwrights at work on some of William's 700 invasion vessels.

However, he still faced great risks. Harold was marching south with all speed – some critics think too much speed – to gather all the forces he had at his disposal. The English fleet, re-manned and refreshed, was according to some accounts about to appear in the Channel and help destroy William's army before it had gained a foothold. But the affair was settled on land. Near the end of a day's bloody fighting on 14 October on the field of Senlac near Hastings, Harold fell, the Normans were victorious and William I was king of England.

KING WILLIAM
An early representation of William I as king.

EQUINE INVADERS

William's army included 7,000 horses. They are shown travelling in ships in several parts of the Bayeux Tapestry. For disembarkation, as contemporary and later pictures show, they went down a ramp in the bows very similar to those of tank landing craft many centuries later.

WILLIAM'S D-DAY
The fleet under way for Pevensey. Note the horses, which look less seasick than some of the army.

15

BUSINESS BY SEA

A barge being loaded at a wharf in a busy commercial scene.

MEDIEVAL TRADER

The Mataro model from the Netherlands Maritime Museum is the only known contemporary, three-dimensional representation of a medieval seagoing craft.

THE FOUR CENTURIES OF Norman, Angevin and Plantagenet rule in England were full of conflict, both external – mainly against France and Scotland – and internal, culminating in the Wars of the Roses. There were natural calamities too, the worst being the Black Death in the middle of the 14th century. Yet during that time, England managed to develop an economy soundly based in agriculture, fisheries and trade.

Trade meant carriage by sea. England needed to import a variety of goods, the most common commodity of all, perhaps, being wine from her possessions in Aquitaine, with Bordeaux the main outlet. In return, England exported grain and fish. Across the North Sea, England offered wool in return for manufactured goods.

The ships for all this trade were primarily sailing craft. They were stoutly built, stood quite high in the water and were of ample beam and depth to carry cargo. They were variously called cogs, nefs or round ships. The most usual unit of capacity was the tun (from which our current term 'ton' or 'tonne' is derived). This was the standard size for the very large barrel in which wine was transported. Some ships had a capacity of up to 300 tuns, but the average was much less.

THE WONDYRCHOUN

This was an early form of beam trawl, about which the English Parliament complained to Edward III in 1377 as a **'lazye and idle kynde of fishing'** which worked **'to the destruction of the fisheries'**. It was banned for the next 300 years.

Cogs were increasingly used for sea warfare as well. Only two open-sea battles are recorded in this period: Dover in 1217 and Les Espagnols sur Mer in 1350. All other engagements were on the older pattern of fights in harbours and estuaries between stationary ships. Only at the very end of the period did gunpowder come into use. The main weapons were bow and arrow, pike, sword and buckler for fighting at close quarters, and stones hurled from high points in the ship (the fore and after 'castles'). The halyards (ropes) of an enemy's sail might be cut, enveloping them in it, and their warriors could be thrown overboard where, encumbered by their armour, they were unlikely to survive.

'Sir Hugh de Berham … has freighted at Bordeaux the cog Our Lady of Lyme … with 93 tuns of wine and 44 tuns of flour to go directly to Newcastle-upon-Tyne.'

A Charter Party of 1323, from the National Maritime Museum, London

Ships were also the only means of transporting armies for overseas expeditions. For his Agincourt campaign, Henry V built a royal fleet of over 30 ships fit for battle, and these were used to dominate the Channel while his army was 'wafted' across for the landing near Harfleur. But after Henry's death the fleet was allowed to decay to nothing.

LIVE FREIGHT
Loading cattle and sheep in a vessel. The mast and sail suggest that a deep-sea voyage lies ahead.

A Nation Goes to Sea

COASTAL DEFENCE

*Typical of Tudor coastal fortifications,
Pendennis Castle faces the sea near
Falmouth, Cornwall.*

IN 1485 RICHARD III's death at Bosworth saw Henry VII become the first Tudor king. The Tudor age, destined to last only 118 years, brought dramatic changes to England and a great increase in her power.

Working through a hand-picked, able and loyal council, Tudor monarchs controlled the country in a way not seen for centuries. England became a nation, no longer a collection of squabbling fiefdoms. Secure in this unity, the English discovered and developed their talents in many ways, matching and often surpassing the nations of Europe in education, law, religion, literature, music and drama. Freed from the worst aspects of feudalism, agriculture, industry and commerce also flourished. In international politics too, the English came of age, responding to challenges and challenging in their turn. Scotland and Ireland were constant preoccupations; France was an early rival and Spain a later one, the Spanish conflict having a strong religious dimension.

In this outburst of vigour and activity, the sea was an increasingly dominant factor. In the time of Henry VII (1485–1509) and even after, primacy at sea fell to the Spanish, Portuguese, Venetians and Genoese. But, under Elizabeth I (1558–1603), English enterprise and latent seafaring skills came to life in a remarkable way. 'Adventure' was the watchword. Drake, Hawkins, the Gilberts, Raleigh, Frobisher, Howard and Grenville became household names.

Their activities went far beyond acquiring treasure or booty. For one thing, English seamanship was critical in the defeat of the Spanish Armada and thus the preservation of England as a sovereign Protestant nation. For another, the voyages of exploration led by Drake, Frobisher and Cavendish and recorded by Hakluyt and Raleigh added vastly to knowledge of the oceans and indeed the world. Finally, the settlements in North America, failures though they were at the time, founded the plantations that later grew into an English-speaking nation across that great continent.

FIRESHIPS AND FIREFIGHT

The Spanish Armada was assailed off Calais, first by fireships and, the next day, by gunfire. The planned invasion of Britain was finally frustrated.

ADVENTURERS ALL

Gentlemen adventurers in their own eyes, pirates to their opponents: Cavendish, Drake and Hawkins (left to right) typified Elizabethan seaborne enterprise.

THE KING'S SHIPS

A WISE PLANNER
Though his son, Henry VIII, took much of the credit, Henry VII laid sound plans for a navy and its armament.

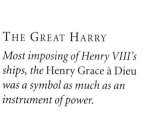

THE GREAT HARRY
Most imposing of Henry VIII's ships, the Henry Grace à Dieu *was a symbol as much as an instrument of power.*

HENRY VII SAW IT as his chief objective to consolidate the power of the Crown. Using able ministers, in particular Cardinal Morton, he took on the two strongest elements in the land, the barons and the Church, diminishing their wealth and influence while increasing his own. While this went on, it was important for him to preserve stable relations abroad, and Henry did this with considerable success. That did not mean, however, that he neglected the national defence. In fact he built up not only a nucleus of 'king's ships', but the beginnings of a naval base at Portsmouth and gun foundries in Kent and Sussex.

That inheritance was built on, with gusto and panache, by his son. Henry VIII was not at all inhibited about external conflicts. No doubt he felt secure enough within the realm to undertake foreign adventures, and he quickly embarked on an almost entirely maritime war with France (1512–14) which seems to have had little strategic purpose. It ended inconclusively, but left the English navy much enhanced and its administration strengthened in a way that was to last.

Henry VIII had strong ideas about his own image, before his own people and those abroad. Great ships were part of it. The towering *Henry Grace à Dieu* (the '*Great Harry*') and *Mary Rose* were built partly as symbolic counters to the big ships of France and Scotland, but they were powerful too, with heavy guns mounted in the broadside, bow and stern. All this contributed to Henry's 'majestas', a favourite word of his, which was never more prominent than at the Field of the Cloth of Gold in 1520 when Henry and the equally charismatic French king, François I, met amidst great pomp.

Sporadic wars against France and Scotland – often both in alliance – continued throughout Henry's reign. In 1545, after a British sally against Boulogne, a French force menaced the Solent and the Isle of Wight. The inconclusive action that followed was most notable for the catastrophic loss of the *Mary Rose*.

Although Henry VIII himself was far more interested in fighting ships, maritime development during his reign was by no means confined to the military sector. Trading activity expanded considerably, in particular across the North Sea and into the Baltic. Founded on wool and cloth exports, it extended to include many other commodities. British penetration of overseas markets was a critical factor in the decline of the Hanseatic League (a monopolistic confederation of northern European trading cities) towards the end of the 16th century.

MAJESTAS
King Henry VIII embarks for the summit meeting with François I at the Field of the Cloth of Gold, 1520.

THE PRIDE OF THE FLEET SINKS

In 1545 Sir Peter Carewe, an eyewitness, recorded: 'The Marye Roose beganne to heele, that is, to leane on the one side … then Sir Gawen Carewe, passing by the Marye Roose, called out to Sir George Carewe, asking how he did? Who answered, that he had a sort of knaves that he coulde not rule. **And it was not long after, that the saide Marye Roose, thus heeling more and more, was drowned, with 700 men which were in her .'**

SUPERIOR FIREPOWER
Now in the Mary Rose Museum at Portsmouth, this culverin shows the rapid advance of weaponry in Tudor times.

TUDOR SHIPS AND SEAMEN

FOR 300 YEARS BEFORE the Tudor age, ship design had developed slowly. But change now became rapid. Guns were becoming common; French galleys already had them in their bows. If English ships were not to be outranged and smashed, a way to fit them had to be found. They were mounted in bow, stern and broadside, pointing out of specially cut gun-ports from strengthened decks. The manoeuvre of ships at sea changed too. The high-sided carrack, typified by the *Mary Rose*, now with up to four masts and a great spread of sail, was imposing but cumbersome, able to make little way to windward. Supporting units to this main fighting ship, sometimes using oars as well as sail, were tried but most were unsuitable for Channel conditions.

SLEEK AND FAST

Evolved in the second half of the 16th century, the race-built galleon was swifter and more easy to handle than any previous design of warship.

NAVIGATIONAL SKILLS

The frontispiece of Wagenhaer's Mariner's Mirror, 1579, shows the skills of steering a course, sounding, charting, astronomical observation and research.

Later in the Tudor period a new design of sailing ship emerged, the 'race-built galleon'. This had a much lower profile than earlier 'great ships', particularly with regard to the bow, which more resembled a galley than the previous high-forecastle craft. The after castle remained in cut-down form, and guns were mounted as before, with due emphasis on bow and stern chasers. This was a nimble and manageable design, able to sail closer to the wind and bring its guns to bear on the enemy with relative ease. It proved itself against the Armada.

One particular difficulty faced by the captains of ships that might have to fight was the relationship between those who worked the ship and those who fought in it. Drake found it acute on his voyage round the world. Indeed he judged that because of it he had to hang his second-in-command. After he did so, he said to the men of his expedition: **'I must have the gentleman to haul and draw with the mariner and the mariner with the gentleman. What! Let us all be of a company.'**

Life at sea could not be anything but hard, given the prevailing harshness of wind and weather, the cramped conditions, the limited facilities for storing and preserving food and the shortage of fresh water. Yet there are indications, particularly from the artefacts recovered from the *Mary Rose*, of a conscious effort by ships' people to make life as tolerable as possible. Personal items such as combs and toothbrushes, and quite sophisticated medical equipment, are at odds with ideas of the rough sailor. Granted that this was one of the top fighting ships of its day, the evidence suggests that Tudor sailors were a resourceful bunch, unlikely to succumb to the challenges the sea or the enemy threw at them.

Meanwhile, merchant vessels continued to be designed for their principal job, carrying cargo. They needed to be armed in order to defend themselves against pirates or lightly-armed privateers, but heavy guns were not in their inventory. Nor were they built for speed or fancy sailing. Reliable and economical carrying of substantial loads was their role. Crews were mostly small in number. Where a warship needed several hundred souls, a merchant ship of comparable size would require only 30 or 40 to manoeuvre the ship and handle the cargo.

NOT SUCH ROUGH SAILORS

Personal possessions recovered from the Mary Rose *included a comb, rosary, coins and beads, indicating the sophistication of her crew.*

THE AGE OF THE FIRST ELIZABETH

THE THRONE THAT ELIZABETH I succeeded to in 1558, on the death of her half-sister Mary I, looked distinctly shaky. Spain, with King Philip II, Mary's husband, at its head, was powerful and hostile. France and Scotland were closely linked by royal ties of blood and marriage, themselves not without claim to the English crown. In addition, previous conflicts meant that neither country was free of resentment towards England.

Over everything loomed questions of religion, and at home these worked to Elizabeth's advantage. The English were in no mood to welcome a return of Catholicism; Mary I's regime had given too sour a taste of it. Moreover, Scottish Protestants looked to England as a necessary, if not much trusted, ally against French attempts to impose an unwelcome religion. This was one of the levers the young queen could use to consolidate her position. More important, however, were

THE CIRCUMNAVIGATOR
Sir Francis Drake, painted by the miniaturist Nicholas Hilliard in 1581 after his voyage round the world.

A QUEEN IN SPLENDOUR
Surrounded by images of nautical exploration and battle, Elizabeth I in her Armada portrait at Woburn Abbey.

LUCKY THIRTEEN

Francis Drake at Tarapaza, Peru, December 1577, recorded, **'On being landed, we found by the sea side a Spaniard lying asleep, who had lying by him 13 bars of silver … we took the silver, and left the man.'** But Drake's circumnavigation was navigational achievement as much as booty-snatching, recorded as such in the chronicles of the time and tracked on the globes constructed by Molyneux in the 1590s. One such globe is still held by the Middle Temple, London.

Elizabeth's strong personality, powerful intellect, political skill and judgement. Sometimes in her reign this last would look like indecision, but more often than not it can now be seen as due thought and consideration, allied to skilful manipulation of the often strong, indeed headstrong, characters with whom she surrounded herself.

Many of those characters were sailors. Even in the early years of the reign Elizabeth was financing ventures into the Atlantic. One motive for this was certainly gain – the royal coffers were dwindling. Without doubt, though, there was impetus from below: networks of adventurers, often from the West Country, saw opportunities in the expanding maritime communities across the Atlantic, still mostly in the hands of Spain and Portugal, and wanted a part of it, by whatever means were available.

Some of these means were more than questionable. For example, John Hawkins conducted three slaving voyages from Africa to the West Indies in the 1560s. The Spaniards protested at the time, not on moral but monopolistic grounds, objecting to interference in lucrative trading patterns which they wanted to reserve for themselves.

'Piratas! Piratas! Piratas!' Count Gondomar, Spanish Ambassador
(Though this protest was made years later, it sums up Spanish outrage at British activities in the Caribbean)

But most of all, they objected to buccaneering and freebooting by English ships. The chief actor in this was Francis Drake. In the early 1570s he had targeted Spanish shipments of bullion from South America with some success. But in 1577 he embarked on a more daring adventure, sailing round the world and taking much Spanish treasure on the way. After a three-year voyage, he was knighted by the queen on the deck of his flagship, the *Golden Hind*.

Drake's achievement was followed by a more straightforward piece of near-piracy six years later, when he returned from the Spanish Main (the Caribbean Sea) laden with loot. By then Spanish patience was exhausted, and Spain and England were to all intents and purposes at war.

A GLOBE OF RECORD
Molyneux's globe (c.1592) not only shows the world as known at the time, but also tracks the voyages of adventurers.

THE SPANISH ARMADA

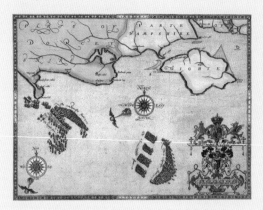

DRUMMING THEM UP THE CHANNEL

The Armada, in an arc formation, was harried up the Channel by Howard of Effingham's ships. Encounters on successive days are shown, first off Portland, Dorset, then off the Isle of Wight.

DRIVEN BY HURT PRIDE, religious fervour and strategic interests in the Netherlands, Philip II of Spain was determined to deal a mortal blow to England's Protestant monarchy. He planned to sail a vast fleet from Spain to link up with the Duke of Parma's forces in the Low Countries. From there, an army of 50,000 would invade England. The menace was clear, and in 1587 Drake was commissioned to launch a pre-emptive attack on Cadiz, where the Armada was preparing. The assault was a stunning success, destroying ships and stores. It was only a raid – 'singeing the King of Spain's beard,' said Drake – but it seriously delayed the Armada's setting out and adversely affected both Spanish morale and finances. Moreover, the designated commander, the able Santa Cruz, died and was succeeded by Medina Sidonia, a good administrator but not a fighting seaman.

The Armada, of some 130 ships, eventually appeared off Cornwall in July 1588. By then the English had about 80 ships available for the Channel, some 40 belonging to the queen and the remainder volunteered by their owners, with more available elsewhere. In overall command was Lord Howard of Effingham, supported by all the foremost captains of the day, including Drake, Hawkins and Frobisher. For a week the English harried the Armada as it made its stately way up the Channel. English ships manoeuvred better than the Spanish and fired their guns much faster. Few captures were made, but the Armada's discipline began to suffer. Things became worse when the fleet eventually arrived off Calais to find that the Duke of Parma's force would take at least a week to embark in full fighting order.

Despite this, the English still saw the situation as critical, and the queen came to Tilbury to make a great rallying speech to her troops. Volunteer forces mustered on shore. Then the naval forces, reinforced by some from the Thames, saw their chance,

A FAMOUS SPEECH

As the Spanish Armada sailed up the English Channel, Queen Elizabeth addressed her troops at Tilbury with these famous words: **'I know I have the body of a weak and feeble woman, but I have the heart and stomach of a king, and of a king of England too; and think foul scorn that Parma or Spain, or any prince of Europe, should dare to invade the borders of my realm.'**

GLORIANA
Nicholas Hilliard's image of Elizabeth I on a gold medal struck to celebrate the defeat of the Armada.

'God blew with his winds, and they were scattered'

Inscription on the Armada medal, 1588

and on the night of 6 August Howard sent in fireships amongst the Spanish fleet. This had a clinching effect. By morning the Armada was scattered along the coastal sandbanks, menaced not only by the English but by an onshore wind. In the ensuing battle, now known as Gravelines, much damage was inflicted by English gunners. The threat was effectively over.

Worse was to befall the Armada. Strong south-westerly winds blew up and lasted much of that autumn. The Spanish ships tried to return to Spain round the north of Scotland, but many were wrecked and only 67 returned. Meanwhile, the English had their reverses too: plague broke out in the fleet and a return to full effectiveness took some time. Nevertheless, the threat from Spain was never again seen as so acute as it had been in the year of the Armada.

THE FIGHT AT SEA
While operationally inaccurate, this picture indicates the confused nature of the up-Channel fight and characteristics of some of the ships.

EXPLORATION AND SETTLEMENT

THE OUTBURST OF ENERGY and enterprise in the last 30 years of Elizabeth's reign sought outlets beyond the country's shores. Nor could it be fully satisfied by warlike or trading exploits that might be profitable but left no permanent mark.

A group of adventurous spirits gathered round Walter Raleigh, including John Dee the mathematician, the geographer Richard Hakluyt, Thomas Hariot the linguist, brothers Humphrey and Adrian Gilbert, John Davis and Martin Frobisher, to develop a wider vision.

'THAT GREAT LUCIFER'

Not everyone approved of the brilliant, thrusting Sir Walter Raleigh, but his leading role in several overseas ventures was undisputed.

LANDING AT ROANOKE

A near-contemporary plan of the arrival of the first settlers near Cape Hatteras, 1585. Note the wrecked ships.

Clearly, the role had to be played out by sea, and had to include not only exploration but actual settlement in other lands. The scope was limited, for Spain and Portugal were already established in the West Indies and Central and South America; Africa was yet too far. The eastern seaboard of North America therefore offered the best opportunity. The Gilberts, Davis and Frobisher concentrated on the north, which had the added attraction of a fabled north-west passage to Japan and China. However, no such passage was found and the attempts took many lives. Raleigh, Hariot and their circle looked further south. In 1584 Raleigh, at the height of power and favour at court, sent out two sea-captains, accompanied by Hariot, to the area of Cape Hatteras. They returned with a glowing report: the place was fertile, the climate superb and the natives friendly. Next year, an expedition set out under Ralph Lane with the aim of permanent settlement in what was to be called Virginia in honour of Elizabeth. But storms destroyed their stores, relations with local tribes worsened and the colonists only just survived the winter. They were glad to take the opportunity of a return passage with Drake the next year.

Raleigh quickly mounted another 'plantation', this time to be further north in Chesapeake Bay and to include women and children, under the artist and mapmaker John White. The plan was sound, but the execution was not. Firstly, the expedition's pilot would not take it beyond Roanoke where the previous one had settled. Secondly, White proved an inadequate leader in other ways. After another dire winter he returned to

POCAHONTAS PLEADS

The first permanent Virginia settlement in 1607 endured many setbacks. Captain John Smith's life was saved by the plea of the Chief's daughter, Pocahontas, on his behalf.

England for help, but by then the Armada threat took up all available resources. The lost colonists, about 100 in number, were never heard of again.

For some 20 years no further plantations took place in North America. Raleigh mounted an expedition much further south in Guyana and made many discoveries, but not the fabled gold of El Dorado that he (and the queen) had expected. However, in the new reign of James I, with Raleigh now discredited, a company was formed to settle Virginia and this, after many hardships and setbacks, finally in 1607 established itself at Jamestown, laying the first permanent foundations for the most powerful nation in the world.

PREMATURE JUDGEMENT

In 1585, Sir Ralph Lane said this of the settlement at Roanoke:

'All ye kingedomes and states of chrystendome … doo not yealde either more good, or more plentyfulle … than is needful or pleasinge for delighte.' Sadly, Sir Ralph's optimism did not survive a hard winter.

A Turbulent Century

THE 17TH CENTURY SAW huge upheavals in Britain and, indeed, in Europe as well. Often these had religious origins, but demands for social justice and national identity were powerful factors too. The Civil War in England, and the Thirty Years' War in Europe, were the most violent episodes, but conflict was a way of life, almost a habit.

Yet during this turbulent century, particularly its second half, trade burgeoned in a dramatic way, not only in volume but in variety. And international trade meant, of course, trade by sea. In the years 1560 to 1689 British shipping expanded sevenfold, while the population only doubled. The old colonial powers, particularly Spain and Portugal, sought to reserve trade from the West Indies and Africa to their own vessels, but the British, and Dutch too, levered themselves into the market. In other parts of the world it was easier for them: in the Mediterranean their activity was marked, and both nations had well-established East India Companies, so the Indian Ocean saw much of them as well.

These massive developments did not happen without force of arms. The great

civil wars and revolutions of England and Europe did not, indeed, see decisive naval action. However, the three Anglo-Dutch Wars in the second half of the century, by far the most intense maritime conflicts fought until then, were a direct result of commercial rivalry between Britain and the Netherlands. They saw much firmer organization of command at sea, and of the protection of trade, than any previous conflicts.

Great progress was also made in the financing and administration of the Navy. The corruption of the early 17th century and the pragmatic measures of its middle years were replaced by a system largely developed by an outstanding civil servant, Samuel Pepys. This was to evolve into the Admiralty of the Georgian era, one of the most powerful departments of state in the land, a necessary basis for the struggle with France that would occupy the next hundred years and more.

THE SOVEREIGN OF THE SEAS
This magnificent ship, painted with her designer Phineas Pett by Lely, typified the majestic 17th-century approach to seafaring. The painting is in the National Maritime Museum, London.

SEA BUSINESS
War and merchant shipping in an estuary: cargo, passenger and warlike operations are all evident in the scene.

ORDERING THE FLEET
As Lord High Admiral, James Duke of York (who later became King James II) codified the Royal Navy's instructions for sailing and fighting.

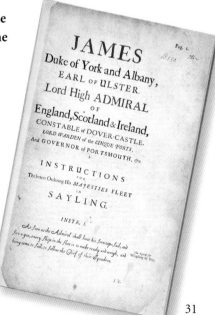

FROM DECAY TO DOMINANCE

HUMILIATION

The Royal Charles *is towed away by the Dutch as a prize after their descent on the Medway, 1667.*

WHILE QUITE WILLING TO spend money on his own state and pastimes, James I was not inclined to lay out finance on wars or maritime adventures. Besides, naval administration was plumbing new depths. Ships and stores were rotten, seamen unpaid and disaffected, officers dissatisfied or corrupt – or both.

⌇

Unsurprisingly, piracy flourished both in home waters and overseas, especially on the north African shore. British and Dutch raids on Barbary bases proved largely ineffective. Equally poor was the Navy's showing in the Thirty Years' War in Europe, a token expedition against Cadiz achieving nothing. The command was untried and incompetent, ships

leaked, provisions went bad and disease was rife. Things began just as poorly under Charles I, with a failed expedition against La Rochelle and the murder of the Duke of Buckingham, who might have put matters to rights. In an effort to assert his sovereignty in waters round the British Isles, Charles built a new fleet. Lacking any parliamentary backing, he financed it with a levy known as Ship Money. The resulting fleet, though costly, was imposing. However the tax became a symbol of Charles's increasingly arbitrary rule, helping to trigger the Civil War which ended in his defeat and execution.

⌇

At the outbreak of the Civil War, the fleet declared for Parliament but had little

> *'It is upon the Navy under the good providence of God that the safety, honour and welfare of this realm do chiefly depend.'*
>
> Articles of War, *1652*

SCHEVENINGEN
A British success of the First Dutch War, recorded by van de Velde the Elder.

influence on events. Things changed when Cromwell finally came to power. The Dutch were the chief problem, because of their potential domination of world trade. In 1652, Cromwell declared war. His ships were heavier and his 'generals-at-sea', under the outstanding Robert Blake, gained several significant victories. Moreover, Dutch trade had to run the gauntlet of the smaller British cruisers and much of it was captured.

Cromwell then turned his sights towards Spain, his plan being to capture Spanish possessions in the West Indies. This had mixed success. An attack on Hispaniola, the main objective, failed; Blake had a brilliant military success at Santa Cruz, but failed to capture the expected booty.

When the monarchy was restored in 1660, Charles II inherited a navy that was strong in ships, but occasionally short on loyalty. However, he soon established his personal sway, embarking on two more Dutch wars, for the issue of maritime dominance was far from settled. In naval terms, neither was as successful as the previous conflict. Some battles were lost, some won, and a dreadful humiliation was suffered when the Dutch raided the Medway in 1667 and towed away the *Royal Charles* as a prize. But Britain's size and power, and in the third war an alliance with France, told in the end. By 1674 the Netherlands were almost exhausted, and though they remained a significant player overseas, their relative decline was certain.

Britain, through these war-torn years, had been steadily building up her own trade: with the Indies east and west, with North America, and in the Mediterranean. It was already the basis for her prosperity, and its protection was already a prime charge on the British state.

GENERAL-AT-SEA
Robert Blake, the most successful of Cromwell's 'generals-at-sea'.

NEW TACTICS AT SEA

During the Dutch Wars the English fleet steadily developed the tactic of fighting in line, so that the heavy guns in the broadside of each ship could all be brought to bear at once, and ships supported one another in battle. This was codified in Fighting Instructions, which were followed – sometimes too rigidly – for the next century and a half.

THE FAMOUS DIARY OF Samuel Pepys, which he wrote between 1660 and 1669, is generally read as a colourful, often racy, account of his time, but Pepys was much more than an observer of the passing show. As Clerk of the Acts and then as Secretary of the Navy, he was a hugely industrious servant of the state, setting in place a system of management that in many aspects remains the model for the running of government departments.

SAMUEL PEPYS

A naval administrator first and foremost, Pepys lives on in his eloquent diaries.

It was mostly about money. The provision of finance for the Navy was uncertain and unpredictable. Between king and Parliament, it was a complex, to-and-fro negotiation that even in wartime was cumbersome and always behindhand. Pepys saw his core task as ensuring that, when money did arrive, it was spent in the service of the Navy, not to line the pockets of individuals. In consequence he made himself master of great swathes of information: about stores, shipbuilding and repairs, victuals, pay, prize money, even the capabilities of individual officers. This he could use to confound corruption, argue for better management, check blatant favouritism and foster promotion on merit.

Pepys did not pretend to be a professional seaman. But, while denying expertise in such things as new sailing rigs and ship construction, he took in enough to know a sound project from an unsound or crooked one. And, if he was not a seaman himself, he recognized the need for the Navy's officers to be professional. He instituted the examination for the rank of

> *'… it is better for us in the navy to have men that do understand the whole …'*   Pepys's diary, 8 December 1667

GREENWICH HOSPITAL
Founded in Pepys's time as a 'hospital for worn-out seamen', Sir Christopher Wren's magnificent design survives today.

LORD HIGH ADMIRAL
In spite of his posturing, James Duke of York did much to help Pepys organize the Royal Navy to face future challenges.

lieutenant, an immensely far-reaching innovation at a time when influence and interest could have run unchecked.

Pepys was a tireless networker. Readers of the diary may note the seemingly endless succession of plays, musical and social events. But so often, in the middle of such activities, Pepys turns out to have met important people like members of the Navy Board or even the king. Every such meeting was turned to account, at least to gain information, often to influence or discuss. This was over and above his more formal conduct of business, which appears little in many editions of the diary, but is prominent in the full version.

Pepys never set out a grand scheme for the Navy, but rather evolved, over 30 years, a pragmatic and flexible method of management. It was no surprise that he weathered several enquiries into his own probity, mainly by simple mastery of the facts. But his tenure of office could not survive the fall of his principal sponsor, now James II, in 1688. The Navy, uncertain which way to jump in any case, was penned in the Thames Estuary by the 'Protestant Wind' that wafted William of Orange to Devon and the Crown. Pepys retired with good sense and good grace.

*'Heart of oak are our ships, jolly tars are our men,
We always are ready: Steady! Boys! Steady!
We'll fight and we'll conquer again and again.'*

Traditional song by David Garrick, 1759

WORLD-BEATING SHIPS

The launch of HMS Cambridge *at Deptford, 1755. Industrial energy and public interest are well displayed.*

THE PERIOD BETWEEN 1690 and 1815 has justly been called the Great Age of Sail. Sailing ships had been used for thousands of years before, and would be used for hundreds of years after; but in no other period did they so dominate world affairs: in trade, in conflict, in exploration, in emerging empires.

Sailing ship technology was at a high and sustained level. There was a generally shared knowledge of the sort of vessel required for any particular task: the roomy cargo craft, the swift dispatch vessel, the stout line-of-battle ship, the nimble frigate and the rakish privateer. Hull forms and sailing rigs were well established. Nowhere was expertise in constructing and handling ships as prominent as in Britain. The Navy might take pride of place, and indeed it, with its

building and dockyards and its stores and victualling organization, was the largest industrial enterprise in the country. But the merchant service, with no government financing, flourished also.

Rivalry with France was the chief political factor of the time. There were periods of peace, but at least five major wars can be counted in little more than a century. With many setbacks and disappointments, British tenacity in the exercise of sea power prevailed, so that in 1815 the scene was set for an extraordinary phenomenon – an expanding maritime empire presided over by a small island off the mainland of Europe.

This was not, of course, achieved without cost. Life at sea was hard, disease-ridden and subject to harsh and sometimes arbitrary discipline. But then life ashore was none too pretty either. In general, ships were at least as humanely conducted as communities on land. The penalties of sea service were not popular, and often accepted reluctantly. But once shaken down, most ships' companies were able to sing *Heart of Oak* without irony.

AN ENDURING SYMBOL

The stem, figurehead and anchor of HMS Victory, *preserved in the Historic Dockyard at Portsmouth.*

THE BEGINNINGS OF MASTERY

A medal commemorating the destruction of the French fleet at La Hougue, 1692.

37

THE RISE OF THE ROYAL NAVY, 1690–1760

OVER A PERIOD OF 70 years, spanning the reigns of William III, Anne and the first two Georges, the Royal Navy advanced from a position of uncertain equality with its rivals to one of established dominance.

It was not done without setbacks. In the first war against France (1689–1712), the British fleet had first to preserve itself while its strength built up, a so-called 'fleet in being' strategy, and suffered a reverse at Beachy Head (1690). But it turned the tables at Barfleur and burnt much of the French fleet at La Hougue (1692). In this war too, Gibraltar withstood a four-year siege and was ceded to Britain in the peace treaty which followed.

At the outbreak of the next conflict 30 years later, Britain dispersed her naval forces unwisely, mounting generally unsuccessful ventures against Spain in the West Indies and a deployment to the Mediterranean. The Battle of Toulon in 1744 was a discreditable affair, with admirals at loggerheads and nothing achieved.

NO RETREAT

The Articles of War were strengthened as a result of the Battle of Toulon (1744). Section XII was an example:

'Every person in the Fleet, who through Cowardice, Negligence, or Disaffection ... shall in time of Action withdraw, or keep back ... or shall not do his utmost ... shall suffer Death.'

It was under this Article that the hapless Admiral Byng was convicted and shot after the loss of Minorca in 1756.

ORDEAL BY FIRE
The French fleet, after its reverse at Barfleur, is destroyed by fireships at La Hougue, 1692.

SCENE OF AN
HISTORIC SIEGE

British forces seized Gibraltar from Spain in 1704 and subsequently withstood a four-year siege. The Rock was formally ceded to Britain in 1713.

The credit of the Navy was greatly boosted by the exploits of Commodore George Anson, who sailed round the world (1740–44). He lost several ships to storm or decay – the shipworm, teredo navalis, had not yet been countered by the copper-bottoming of hulls – and many men to disease, but captured a vastly rich treasure in a Spanish Manila galleon and opened windows on the world that had been closed to the British for a century and a half. Anson later became a superb naval administrator, responsible for forging the Navy into an even more effective instrument in the next war with France.

It was this, known as the Seven Years' War, that saw the rise of British naval mastery to the plateau it occupied for the next 150 years. It began badly with the loss of Minorca, but the generally maritime strategy of William Pitt the Elder, and the operational expertise of admirals such as Hawke, Boscawen and Saunders, bore fruit. In 1759 – the 'wonderful year' of the song *Heart of Oak* – Hawke and Boscawen won decisive victories at sea, Saunders helped Wolfe's army to win at Quebec and establish British rule in Canada, and Robert Clive with British naval support secured a large part of India. This has justly been called 'the first world war'. It was indeed as widespread as that, and Britain ended it with huge advantages she did not have before – not least the sense that to her the sea was not a barrier, but the road to further opportunities.

NAVIGATOR, FIGHTER
AND ADMINISTRATOR

Admiral George, Lord Anson, went round the world in 1740–44, won a major battle in 1747 and then masterminded naval development.

39

LIFE AT SEA UNDER SAIL

ALTHOUGH KNOWLEDGE and consciousness of the sea was widespread in the Great Age of Sail, most seamen came from coastal counties. Fishermen's sons would probably follow their fathers, deep-sea sailors likewise. Merchant service numbers remained constant at around 40,000 through the century, but the Royal Navy, about 16,000 in peace, needed 70,000 or more in war. Press gangs ashore, and naval ships afloat, were authorized to compel seamen to serve on board warships, and often landsmen would be brought in too. Officers were a different breed; often they were younger sons of substantial families entering the Navy at an early age, with the prospect of acquiring status, maybe honour, and even prize money.

Whatever their motives for being there, men at sea could expect a tough life. However professionally a ship might be constructed, fitted out and handled, the sea was unforgiving. Voyages might last months and span half the globe, so every sort of weather and sea could be expected. Calm was as dangerous as storm; a ship in the Doldrums could stay becalmed for weeks, with victuals and, worse, water running low. Storms took a more dramatic toll. The only way of taking in sail, essential for the safety of the ship, was for men to go aloft and physically gather it in. These were the most skilled

JACK

A sailor bringing up his hammock, sketched by Gabriel Bray in 1775.

THE PRESS GANG

Collings's cartoon illustrates the lengths to which the Navy went to man the fleet in wartime.

seamen, the topmen, but even they sometimes lost their footing and plunged to their death.

⁓

The greatest killer of all, though, was disease. Typhus, or gaol fever, often struck at the beginning of wars, when the prisons were scoured for naval recruits. Yellow fever was a particular scourge in the West Indies and Africa. But the disease most typical of long sea voyages was scurvy, a wasting ailment with unusually disgusting symptoms such as loss of teeth and foul breath. The antidote, a diet including citrus fruit and green vegetables, took a century and more to establish. Good captains instinctively procured these things as a matter of course whenever there was an opportunity. Unimaginative ones did not.

⁓

The dangers and conditions of service meant that sailors, merchant and naval, were a fairly unruly lot. Drunkenness was a common offence, along with insubordination and neglect of duty. The most common punishment was flogging, with the miscreant lashed to a grating and the cat-o'-nine-tails, a rope lash with several knotted strands, administered by a boatswain's mate. It was brief but brutal. One or two captains, too free with the lash to the point of tyranny, were murdered by enraged or mutinous crews. Most, though, were measured in discipline and humane in their treatment of ships' companies. Many crews would follow their captains anywhere, and took immense pride in the performance of their ships, in peace and war.

PREVENTING SCURVY
James Lind published his treatise on the role of citrus fruit in the prevention of scurvy in 1757, but his analysis was subjected to ill-conceived experiments for three more decades.

'No man will be a sailor who has contrivance enough to get himself into a jail; for being in a ship is being in a jail, with the chance of being drowned …'

Dr Samuel Johnson, 1759

THE CAT
Miscreants were strapped to a grating before being flogged with the cat-o'-nine-tails.

41

THE EAST INDIA COMPANY

THE NABOB

Warren Hastings, Governor General of India, depicted by an Oudh artist, 1782. Historically, a nabob was a European who made a fortune in the East.

HOMEWARD BOUND

East Indiamen and traders in the Sunda Strait, between Java and Sumatra.

THE PORTUGUESE, AND THEN the Dutch, had been the pioneers in establishing themselves in the Indian Ocean and beyond, in the 15th and 16th centuries. The potential prizes were great. Spices were in huge demand in Europe to flavour and preserve food in the days before refrigeration was invented. So were silks, damasks and porcelain. Trading opportunities were many, and potential profits enormous.

The British East India Company was formed in 1600 to trade between the East and the home country. It was later supported by both Cromwell and the restored Stuarts. Portuguese interest dwindled. While the Dutch remained dominant in the East Indies, in the sub-continent British influence steadily increased. Mumbai (Bombay) was acquired as a major trade centre in 1668. Nearly 100 years later Robert Clive and Warren Hastings checked French initiatives, and 40 years after that the Wellesleys decisively tightened the British hold on India. The East India Company was at its height, commanding more wealth and income than the home state itself. It was not until the 1850s, with the aftermath of the Indian Mutiny, that the British government formally took over the rule of the subcontinent.

All this needed an efficient trading fleet, and the East India Company had some 75 vessels, replenished by new building in British shipyards. Ships were well-found,

One risk, for the seamen at any rate, was impressment by the Royal Navy, particularly in wartime. But Indiamen sometimes used their arms against the enemy too. The most celebrated action was that of Commodore Nathaniel Dance, when with a convoy of 16 ships he held off a force of the French Navy under Admiral Linois in 1804. This was rightly hailed as an example of British skill and tenacity. Dance got an annuity of £500 for this action. In general, the East India Company generated riches for its members and, incidentally, for Britain as a whole.

'Neither did we want milk, having a fine Goat that supplied us with it all the passage.'

James Barlow, passenger in the Indiaman Boscawen, 1749

handsome, substantial, and armed, with ample crews. These 'Indiamen' were generally owned by syndicates, mostly of Company people following Company orders and customs.

Chief among these were the 'ships' husbands' – effectively, their shore managers – and the captains. Their pay was nothing special by the standards of the time. It was the profit from their private ventures – import and export in the ships on their own account – that mattered. It was said that captains could make enough from three voyages to retire in comfort, and officers and crew did equally well on a smaller scale. It was no wonder that in spite of the risks of the sea, and of piracy and of enemy action in war, service with 'John Company' (as the company was familiarly known) was much sought after.

A DOUBLE IMPRESSMENT

The Indiaman *Castle Eden* returned to England in 1808 under the escort of HMS *Monmouth*. Before land was sighted, she was ordered by the *Monmouth* to provide five men for the Navy, and another 25 on anchoring in the Downs off Deal. After protests, the *Monmouth* relented, taking only three, but in the Downs another naval ship pressed 22. The naval lieutenant who was in charge rebuffed all argument by saying, **'Let them look out that's got the watch'.**

THE SLAVE TRADE

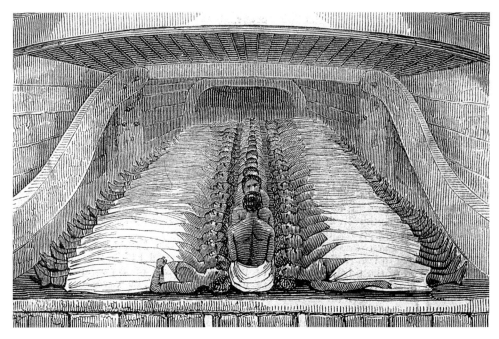

This sketch of the appallingly cramped accommodation in the hold of a slave ship looks improbably diagrammatic but much other evidence confirms it as being accurate.

'I could not sleep ... without dreaming of scenes of depredation and cruelty on the injured shores of Africa ...'

William Wilberforce,
March 1805

THE SLAVE TRADE, which was dreadful enough in principle, was even more repellent in practice. Voyages took a triangular form. Slave ships sailed from Bristol or Liverpool with a cargo of cheap goods. In West Africa these (or occasionally money) were exchanged for slaves, through agents who negotiated with local chiefs or professional traders, most of them Arabs. With their human cargo the ships then sailed for the West Indies or, in later years, the southern USA.

During this 'middle passage', which might last many weeks, conditions were appalling. Slaves were confined, often in shackles, lying close together without proper sanitation. The stench of a slave ship was said to be unmistakable and unforgettable. Some captains, perhaps with a better price for their slaves in mind, would allow batches of them on deck for exercise. Others were less humane. Death rates were often as high

as a quarter. The survivors were sold at markets in Barbados or further west, to work in the plantations. Slave ships would then embark a cargo, generally of sugar, for the voyage home.

The slave trade was first established by Spain and Portugal to their colonies in Brazil and the Caribbean. The first Englishman to become involved was John Hawkins, who embarked on three voyages during the 1560s. Britain showed no further interest until nearly a century later, by which time she had acquired a good deal of North America and also the island of Jamaica. In those places, cotton and sugar production required a very large workforce of strong men used to hot conditions. Africans proved ideal, and any moral scruples gave way to greed and commercial interests. Others convinced themselves that Africa was a benighted, cruel continent, and that those transferred to the West Indies or

THE TYRANNY OF SUGAR

A slave cutting cane, 1799. The atmosphere of such pictures reflected the sentiments leading to the abolition of the trade.

WEST INDIAN SLAVERY

Breaking up the land in Antigua, 1823. Though Britain abolished the trade in 1807, slavery in British possessions persisted until 1834.

America would there lead happier lives under benign masters, with the benefit moreover of a Christian environment. By the middle of the 18th century Britain was shipping some 50,000 slaves a year across the Atlantic.

Gradually, however, towards the end of the 18th century, other sentiments gained ground. Evangelists and politicians, Ramsay, Clarkson, Wilberforce and Pitt the Younger, banded together to lobby against the trade, its inhumanity and its hypocrisy. In 1807, after many checks and setbacks, the House of Commons passed the Bill for abolition of the trade; Britain was the first country to do so. For the next 40 years, the Royal Navy patrolled the west coast of Africa, at first only to enforce the prohibition against British ships but steadily extending it to other nations as these fell into line. It was, at least, some salve to a nation's conscience. But the cost in sailors' lives through disease was high.

WILLIAM WILBERFORCE

A truly great man, as MP for Hull he fought a long, brave and tireless campaign to abolish the British slave trade.

PIRACY, THE TAKING – by force or threat of force – of a ship's cargo, or the ship itself, or its people, or all three, was a crime of the sea from the very earliest times. Around Britain, the Saxons practised it and, later, the English in the Channel. Sometimes it was given legitimacy as a 'reprisal' for a previous wrong, but mostly it was outside the law, even though authority could do little about it.

With better regulation of British waters the focus of piracy shifted in the 17th century to the Caribbean Sea and Indian Ocean. By then sea trade was widespread, rich pickings were available, and naval patrols few. Moreover, there was often a patriotic excuse: 'we are only plundering the Spaniards/French/Dutch'. But in fact the pirates preyed on everyone. Male or female – Mary Bonney is as famous a name as Henry Morgan – they were a long way from the romantic image of the pirate, wronged in his or her youth and seeking redress by robbing the unjustly rich. A few, including the notorious Captain Kidd, fitted this picture, but much more typical was Edward Teach, the famous Blackbeard, who set out to terrorize the West Indies and Eastern seaboard of America. With fireworks in his hair and a

PIRATE FLAGS

Variations on the theme of the infamous 'skull and crossbones'.

BLACKBEARD

The fearsome Edward Teach, most deliberately menacing of pirates, whose reign of terror was ended in 1718.

'Ships of his Majestie ... have express orders to take, sink, burn or otherwise destroy such pirates as may infest those seas ...'

The Lords of Admiralty to Lord Newcastle, 5 March 1725

THE SMUGGLERS

By the contemporary artist George Morland, this gives an authentic picture of surreptitious trading.

permanently bloodied sword, he succeeded for some years but was eventually brought to book by Lieutenant Maynard, who displayed his severed head on the bowsprit of HMS *Pearl* as she returned to harbour.

Pirates were regarded then, as they still are, as the enemies of all seagoers. It was not so with smugglers. In the age of sail, one of the chief ways of raising money for the government was customs duty, which was levied on imports of goods that people thought particularly desirable such as tea, silks, lace and liquor. The majority of the population resented these impositions and tried to get round them by whatever ways were available. Smuggling was one of those ways, so those who practised it were not generally unpopular. Since the nearest land from which goods might come was France, much smuggling took place on the Channel coast. Kent saw most activity, with well-organized seafarers supported by gangs – and sometimes the local gentry – ashore. But farther west the effort was almost as intense, and the local community even more involved. Smugglers used all sorts of devices to conceal their cargoes, sunken tubs being the method of choice for brandy.

Customs officers had a rough time. Though well supported by legislation and equipped with special craft, they ran all sorts of risks – including murder – and it was not until the 1820s, with the introduction of better surveillance and communication, that they began to gain the upper hand. The introduction of freer trade in the middle of the century removed the main attractions of smuggling, and its widespread practice dwindled away.

CHARTING A TRUE COURSE

AN EARLY CHART

Though the shape of the Americas is recognizable on this early 17th-century chart, it could by no means be used for precise navigation.

THE NATURAL INCLINATION OF most early seafarers was to stay in sight of land that they knew. When they set out to cross a wider stretch of sea, they could set a compass course and be guided to safety by known landmarks and other characteristics such as the sea bottom, identifiable by letting out the indispensable lead-line, 'armed' with grease.

However, when ocean voyages were undertaken, the unknowns and risks were altogether greater, and sailors had to use astronomical observations. Finding the latitude was not difficult. Each day, when the sun reached its highest elevation, its

MEASURING ALTITUDE

The sextant supplanted earlier instruments for observing the altitude of sun, moon and stars.

altitude was measured by a sextant or similar instrument, and the latitude could be readily calculated by applying data from an almanac. The latitude of major ports was known, so the simplest way to reach them was to sail along their latitude until one arrived. Arab and Chinese navigators had done this for hundreds of years; 'almanac' is an Arabic word.

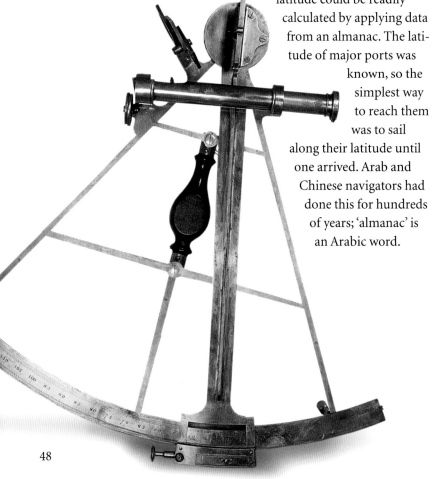

But, for ocean voyages of exploration or trade, safety and efficiency demanded that the longitude should be known also. This was a more difficult problem, because the rotation of the earth on its axis brings time into the equation. In effect, to determine the longitude an observer has to know the time at a fixed meridian – in Britain this was set at the meridian of Greenwich – and then compare it with an astronomical observation which, by reference to the

48

A DEFINING TIMEPIECE
John Harrison's superb fourth chronometer was the culmination of his craftsmanship and the most practical solution of the longitude problem.

is hard, and the calculation is time-consuming. Nevertheless the lunar method was used, particularly by the East India Company, for many years.

The other method was to make a clock that could stand the motion of the sea and remain accurate for long periods. Over many years in the mid 18th century John Harrison perfected his chronometers. Finally, with his fourth, he produced a timepiece so reliable, as well as beautiful, that Captain James Cook used and praised an exact copy on his great voyages. Gradually the chronometer superseded all other means of keeping time at sea. Harrison eventually was paid most of the reward that had been offered long before by the Board of Longitude for the solution to the problem. But credit must also go to the astronomers, particularly Nevil Maskelyne, Astronomer Royal (1765–1811) who produced the almanacs without which accurate navigation by the sun, moon and stars would not have been possible.

almanac, will establish the local time at his or her position. And that gives one the longitude.

The difficulty was to know the Greenwich time. There were no digital clocks, radio time signals or satellite systems, but there was an astronomical way. Because the moon appears to move much faster round the heavens than any other body, the angle between it and sun, stars and planets is changing quite rapidly, so rapidly that if accurately measured it can, after calculation, give the Greenwich time. The difficulty is practical: measurement of that angle from the deck of a rolling and pitching ship

'Whereas … nothing is so much wanted and desired at sea, as the discovery of the Longitude …'

Preamble to the first Longitude Act, 1713

NEW ZEALAND CHARTED

An overlay of Captain Cook's survey with a modern chart shows the extraordinary accuracy he achieved.

BORN IN YORKSHIRE IN 1728 and brought up in the East Coast coaling trade, James Cook volunteered for the Royal Navy, becoming a Master – a warrant officer with special responsibility for navigation. He came to notice by making surveys on the coast of Canada and in 1768, still nominally a lieutenant, was selected to conduct a voyage of exploration in the Pacific. This was to include an important astronomical observation from the island of Tahiti. But his confidential instructions told him to seek the great continent then thought to girdle the earth far to the south, and to take possession, in the name of King George, of any lands discovered. Over the next 12 years Captain Cook made three voyages to the Pacific, disproving the existence of a habitable southern continent but charting New Zealand, most of the east coast of Australia, much of the west coast of North America and many of the Pacific islands.

Cook took with him on his voyages a team of talented people: astronomers, botanists, artists and draughtsmen. Of these, Joseph Banks, who went only on the first voyage, later achieved fame as a naturalist and became President of the Royal Society. Cook set the highest standards of accuracy in survey, of endurance in adversity and of care for his ship's company. His common sense in providing a varied diet including citrus fruit and vegetables, and an insistence on cleanliness, ensured that his ship had no serious cases of scurvy. Unhappily, the full significance of his policies was not recognized for another 30 years.

'That, Captain Bligh, that is the thing … I am in hell!'

Fletcher Christian, mate of the Bounty, when casting Bligh adrift

MUTINY ON THE BOUNTY

Some years after Cook's last voyage, HMS *Bounty* called at Tahiti on another expedition. William Bligh, her captain, was a volatile man and alienated his officers and crew. They cast him adrift in an open boat with a handful of supporters. He navigated brilliantly to reach the East Indies 5,000 kilometres (3,000 miles) away, but his subsequent career was marred by further friction with subordinates. Meanwhile, the mutineers reached Pitcairn Island where some of their descendants live to this day.

His relations with the populations of the Pacific islands, with attitudes to property and ownership so different from those that British people held, were generally courteous but sometimes demanded firmness. This he exercised with great judgement in his first and second voyages. He was less measured during the third. In February 1779 when he had to return to Hawaii through storm damage, the people who had previously received him as a demigod turned against him. When a quarrel escalated, they killed him on the shore.

All Cook's ships were designed on the lines of the Whitby colliers he knew so well: sturdy, well-found and comfortable in a seaway. His first, HM Bark *Endeavour*, was built in 1764 and extensively refitted for the voyage, and the same procedure was used for the *Resolution* in the second and third voyages. In the 1990s an Australian foundation, with support from the National Maritime Museum, Greenwich, financed and supervised a reconstruction of the *Endeavour*. This superbly built and managed vessel circumnavigated the British Isles in 1997, returning to Britain on occasions since then.

THE SOUTH SEAS
Tahitian war canoes painted by Cook's artist, William Hodges.

A PEACEABLE HERO
James Cook's three Pacific voyages showed superb leadership, navigation and seamanship.

SET ADRIFT
The Bounty *mutiny as depicted on a cigarette card of the 1920s.*

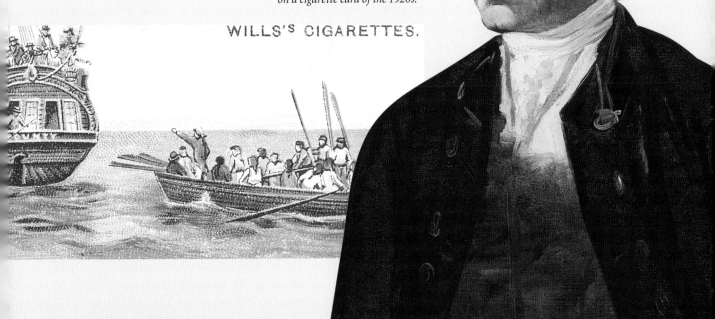

WILL'S CIGARETTES.

THE 1760S SAW BRITAIN dominant at sea and powerful across the world. However, the colonies of North America were resentful of British rule and taxation, and in 1775 the War of American Independence began. Britain had no European allies, so France could help America fully. Britain's fleets were sometimes poorly handled, and her unsupported land forces had to surrender at Yorktown. The United States of America were established.

In 1793, alarmed by the French Revolution and the subsequent 'Reign of Terror' in Paris, Britain and many continental powers declared war on the new French Republic. This looked at first like an 18th-century war: British military enterprises in the West Indies and India, minor threats of invasion through Ireland. But with the emergence of Napoleon as leader and eventually emperor, the conflict became much sterner, being regarded in Britain as a war of survival against tyranny.

Dominant on land in Europe, Napoleon sought to open a route to India by way of Egypt, but he was frustrated by Nelson's victory at the Nile (1798), British landings and success in the Delta, and Captain Sidney Smith's defence of the fortress of Acre in what was then Palestine.

So Napoleon's Empire was restricted to Europe. The Royal Navy dominated the oceans, capturing ships and cargoes in

SURRENDER AT YORKTOWN

Britain's naval ascendancy was not enough to succeed in keeping her American colonies; the USA's independence was acknowledged in 1782.

French service and ramming home its supremacy at Camperdown (1797), Copenhagen (1801), Trafalgar (1805) and many lesser actions. Napoleon was forced to institute his 'continental system', virtually turning the continent of Europe into a closed economic community. But too many people in Europe wanted goods from outside, and the British set up a system that supplied them – to British advantage. Meanwhile Wellington, supported by British sea power, was steadily advancing through Spain to threaten Napoleon's southern flank.

Increasingly frustrated by European non-compliance with his continental system's rules, Napoleon turned on Russia, in his eyes one of the chief culprits. His expedition went disastrously wrong and, much weakened, he abdicated and retired to Elba. Escaping from there, he had a further 'Hundred Days' of glory in 1815, but was defeated at Waterloo and surrendered to Captain Maitland who, in HMS *Bellerophon*, was blockading the French naval port of Rochefort. He was exiled to St Helena and died there in 1821.

The French Revolutionary and Napoleonic Wars saw the Royal Navy at its operational zenith. It was the chief instrument of British power. Though British armies fought well throughout the wars, they could not have reached any overseas theatres without naval support, and the Navy's control of sea traffic played a decisive part in weakening Napoleon's Empire. The only significant naval reverses suffered were in the war of 1812–14 against the United States,

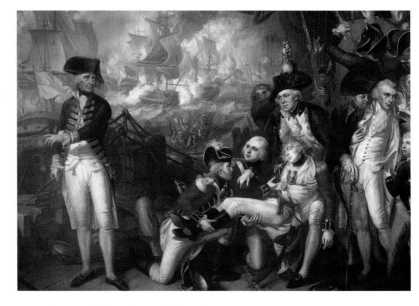

several British ships being defeated in single-ship actions. This unnecessary war ended with no advantage to either side.

THE GLORIOUS FIRST

In the 1790s, the Royal Navy gained early victories against revolutionary France, notably on 1 June 1794.

> '*Those far-distant, storm-beaten ships, on which the Grand Army never looked, stood between it and the dominion of the world.*'
>
> Alfred Thayer Mahan, The Influence of Sea Power upon the French Revolution and Empire

CAMPERDOWN

The Dutch, allied to France, were defeated in October 1797, shortly after British naval mutinies against corruption and mismanagement.

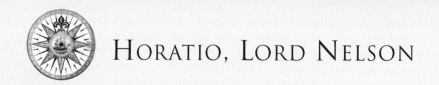

HORATIO, LORD NELSON

'All agree: there is but one Nelson.' Earl St Vincent, 1798

BIRD'S-EYE VIEW

Nelson's statue on top of his famous column in Trafalgar Square, London.

HORATIO NELSON WAS BORN at Burnham Thorpe, Norfolk, in 1758, the younger son of a country parson. Some naval relations gave him the necessary 'interest' to join the Navy as an officer, and his ability and dedication marked him for rapid promotion; he was a post captain at 24. During his service in the West Indies he married Frances Nisbet, a widow with a son also destined for the Navy.

Nelson greatly distinguished himself ashore and afloat in the first four years (1793–97) of the war in the Mediterranean. At Calvi in Corsica, he lost almost all the sight of his right eye. A much-needed victory off Cape St Vincent in 1797, under Sir John Jervis, was achieved largely due to the initiative and courage of Nelson, who was knighted and promoted to the rank of rear admiral.

Later in the year he was instructed to assault Tenerife in the Azores. Nelson was over-confident, the Spaniards robust, and the weather unfavourable. The operation failed. Nelson's right arm was shattered and only the quick action of his stepson Josiah prevented his bleeding to death. But his reputation now was such that this reverse did not prevent his commanding

NELSON AT CAPE ST VINCENT

Commodore Nelson in the 74-gun *Captain*, towards the rear of the British line, observed that a part of the opposing Spanish fleet was in a position either to reinforce the main body or to escape. He promptly left the line – a cardinal offence by the fighting instructions of the day – and made for the separated ships, many of them more powerful than his own. Several other British ships came to his support, and the *Captain*, much shattered, nevertheless boarded and captured first the *San Nicolas* and, via her, the *San Josef*; the two ships' combined gun-power was three times the *Captain*'s. The press hailed the exploit as 'Nelson's patent bridge for boarding First-rates' – a phrase Nelson was not reluctant to quote.

a strong British squadron next year in the Mediterranean, and this led to his most complete victory at Aboukir Bay (known as the Battle of the Nile; 1798), where he virtually annihilated a French fleet of over a dozen ships.

Nelson, now a viscount, returned to Naples where he became involved not only with the murky politics of the area, but personally with Lady Hamilton, the wife of the British ambassador. He (and she) returned to England in 1800–01, where Nelson – shunned at Court – nevertheless went as second in command of a squadron sent to Denmark to force the Danes to abandon their armed

neutrality, which harmed British interests. This he achieved at the Battle of Copenhagen, a tough slogging match.

When the Peace of Amiens broke down in 1803 Nelson was again sent to the Mediterranean to watch the Toulon fleet. His two hard years there, with a brief respite (in the company of Lady Hamilton) in England in the summer of 1805, ended with his greatest victory at Trafalgar over a combined French and Spanish fleet. Nelson died in the moment of victory, shot by a sniper from the fighting tops of the *Redoutable*.

Renowned as Britain's greatest fighting admiral, Nelson has generated a vast amount of literature covering a whole range of opinions. On some aspects of his abilities, though, there is general agreement: his inspiring leadership, his attacking spirit, and his tactical originality. These are commemorated in many naval circles on Trafalgar Night, 21 October.

THE BATTLE OF THE NILE

The spectacular explosion of the French flagship L'Orient at the height of the battle. An awestruck silence followed for 10 minutes.

EMMA, LADY HAMILTON

Both colourful characters, Nelson and Lady Hamilton were closely involved for the last seven years of his life.

A HERO AT REST

Nelson's mask taken after his death at the Battle of Trafalgar, 21 October 1805.

55

HMS VICTORY

HMS *VICTORY* WILL FOREVER be associated with Nelson at Trafalgar, but by the time of that battle she had already given distinguished service for 40 years.

The largest British warship of her time, *Victory* was ordered in 1758 amid great public interest. However, with the coming of peace in 1763 the hull languished on the slipway at Chatham before finally being launched in May 1765. This period of waiting allowed her massive oak timbers to become fully seasoned, and helped her future survival.

With over 100 guns and 850 men, *Victory* was destined to be a flagship and bore the flags of many admirals, among them Sir John Jervis at Cape St Vincent in 1797. On 18 May 1803, after *Victory*'s refit at Chatham, Vice Admiral (and Viscount) Horatio Nelson embarked in her for his long vigil, first off Toulon and then in the Atlantic to prevent any concentration of the French and Spanish fleets that could threaten the British Isles with invasion. No one knew better than Nelson that the best way of completing this mission was to bring them to action, but his counterpart, Villeneuve, eluded him for many months until the combined fleet was finally forced into Cadiz. Meanwhile Nelson prowled outside.

Stung by the knowledge that Napoleon was about to replace him, Villeneuve determined to offer battle, and the fleets met on 21 October 1805 off Cape Trafalgar, 33 French-Spanish ships of the line against 27 British. Nelson's daring plan was to sail in two columns at right angles to the enemy line to cut it and 'bring on a pell-mell action'. *Victory* led the windward line and passed astern of Villeneuve's flagship, the *Bucentaure*, shattering her stern with her first broadside, killing 200 men, disabling 20 guns and effectively putting her out of action.

IN ACTIVE SERVICE

HMS Victory *is still a fully commissioned ship, flying the flag of the Second Sea Lord and Commander-in-Chief of the Royal Navy's Home Command.*

The French *Redoutable* offered resistance and a sniper in her fighting tops shot Nelson down. The admiral was carried below and died some hours later, but not before he had received news of a complete victory. Nineteen ships of the French-Spanish fleet were captured, but many were lost in a subsequent storm, and only four reached Britain.

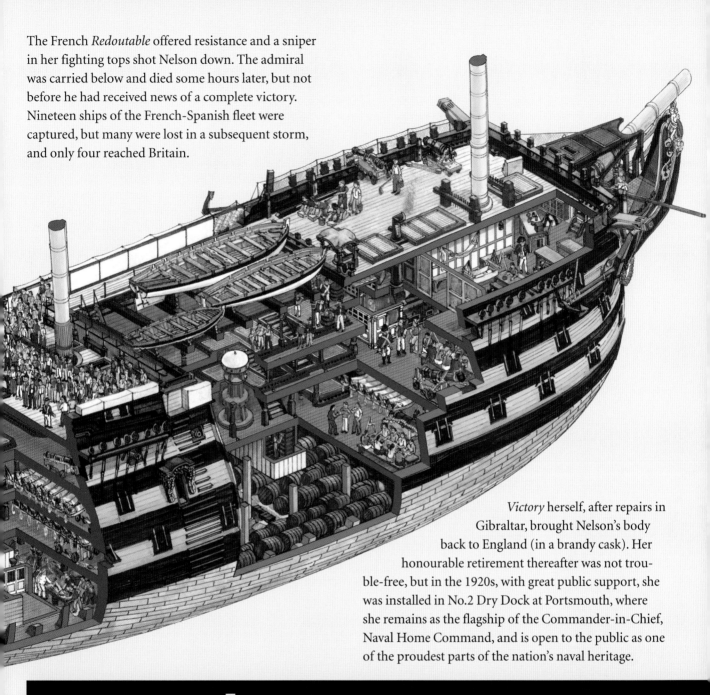

Victory herself, after repairs in Gibraltar, brought Nelson's body back to England (in a brandy cask). Her honourable retirement thereafter was not trouble-free, but in the 1920s, with great public support, she was installed in No.2 Dry Dock at Portsmouth, where she remains as the flagship of the Commander-in-Chief, Naval Home Command, and is open to the public as one of the proudest parts of the nation's naval heritage.

THE BIRTH OF AN IMMORTAL PHRASE

As the *Victory* closed on the enemy, Nelson announced, **'I'll now amuse the Fleet with a signal.' Turning to his Flag Lieutenant, he said, 'Mr Pasco, I wish to say to the Fleet "England confides that every man will do his duty."'** The lieutenant ventured to suggest that by substituting **'expects' for 'confides'**, the signal would be more quickly sent, since 'expects' was represented by three flags while 'confides' would have had to be spelled out. 'That will do, Pasco,' replied the admiral. 'Make it directly.' In this curious way, the famous phrase was born.

PRIZES!

ADMIRALTY JUDGE

Sir William Scott, later Lord Stowell, gave over 5,000 prize judgments in the Admiralty Court from 1798 to 1828. The awarding of prize money for captured ships continued until 1945, though by then pooled into a single fund.

CAPTURING SHIPS TO SELL them and their cargoes started in early times as out-and-out piracy, but governments began to adopt it as an act of economic warfare and by the 16th century the idea of 'lawful prize' was established: a capture, if justified by the situation at the time, should be 'condemned' in court. The first judge of the English Admiralty Court had the unlikely name of Julius Caesar.

Prize-taking became well established in the Dutch Wars (1652–54; 1665–67; 1672–78), but the government took a large part of the proceeds and the incentives for captors were not great. In 1708, however, the Cruizers and Convoys Act made over the rights of the Crown to the captors, whether naval ships or privateers operating under 'letters of marque'.

British warships and privateers took great numbers of prizes in the wars that followed. Enemy warships might fetch a lot of money, including 'head money' for each member of the enemy crew. Merchant ships could be richly laden, but others were scarcely worth the taking. For recaptures, a grateful owner was expected to pay salvage.

Captors did have to pay the expenses incidental to capture, court appearance and sale. Rumours about rapacious agents and court officials were rife (and are often reproduced in current fiction), but analysis of the records suggests these were mostly unfounded. At home a captor could expect to get about 80 per cent of the gross proceeds – not a bad return. On some overseas stations, corrupt practices existed in the Vice Admiralty Courts, but captors indulged in some free-and-easy goings-on themselves, including taking ransom money, a practice forbidden under British law.

Distribution of the net proceeds was regulated according to a precisely laid-down scale. The captain got a quarter of the whole. This was a high proportion, but his was the sole responsibility. If he made an unlawful capture, such as taking the ship of a neutral country, resulting in its return, he was liable for damages. The flag officer on the station got an eighth, and several admirals made fortunes thereby. Officers and crew took the rest, in descending order. For the last few years of the Napoleonic Wars a more equitable scale, rewarding middle-ranking ratings, was introduced.

PRIVATEER CAPTURE

HMS Wolverene *captures a French privateer. Such actions helped to protect British merchant shipping.*

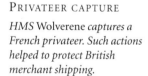

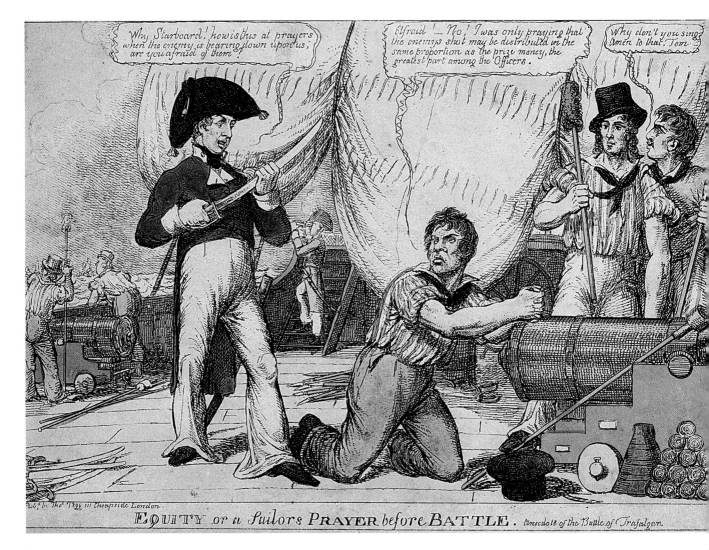

Why Starboard! how is this at prayers when the enemy is bearing down upon us; are you afraid of them?

Afraid! — No! I was only praying that the enemys shot may be distributed in the same proportion as the prize money, the greatest part among the Officers.

Why don't you sing Amen to that, Tom.

EQUITY or a Sailors PRAYER before BATTLE. *Anecdote of the Battle of Trafalgar.*

AN EXCHANGE OF VIEWS

Officer: What! On your knees before the enemy; are you afraid?
Sailor: Afraid? No, I was praying that the enemy's shot may be distributed in the same proportion as the prize money, the greater part to the officers.

With pay for all members of the Navy at a low level, prize money was a tremendous incentive for officers and ratings alike. Often they were disappointed even if a prize was taken – the average gross 'take' for a merchant capture was about £2,500 – but hope always beckoned. It was customary for officers to disclaim interest in prizes: 'I never cared much about riches', wrote Edward Pellew, who by 1815 had netted a cool £300,000. But in fact no one, not even Nelson, not even Collingwood, was immune.

A LUCRATIVE CAPTURE

The captain of HMS *Brilliant* recorded in his log on 28 December 1798: **'Fresh gales and hazey. Saw a strange sail to windward gave chace Boarded her made her a Prize and detained her supposing her to be a Dutch Indiaman under Danish colours called the *Eenrom*.'** The *Eenrom* was condemned as lawful prize in the Admiralty Court and netted nearly £24,500 for the captors.

LAND HO!

Sailor songs, suits and sentiments were a prominent part of Victorian and Edwardian culture. This is the cover of the sheet music for a popular song of the late 19th century.

SS GREAT BRITAIN

Designed by the great engineer Isambard Kingdom Brunel, this steam-powered, propeller-driven, transatlantic passenger ship, imaginatively preserved at Bristol, typified Victorian maritime enterprise.

FROM THE END OF the Napoleonic Wars in 1815, Britain's dominance at sea was established for the rest of the century. It was founded on, and safeguarded by, possession of a much stronger navy than any potential rival; challenges were repulsed with relative ease. In part, this was through the scientific and industrial lead that Britain held throughout the century. If an opponent produced a novel idea, Britain had enough capacity to adopt it and quickly outbuild its rival, usually with a more robust system.

Technology developed rapidly. In 1815 there were almost no steam-powered vessels; ships were made of wood and used smooth-bore cannon. By the end of the century steam had almost completely replaced sail, warships were built of steel and were often armour-plated, and were equipped with rifled long-range artillery, throwing explosive shells. This was a real revolution in naval affairs and the British were out in front, always in quantity and generally in quality.

That situation was matched, sometimes led, by the merchant marine. The expansion of British commercial interests around the globe caused an upsurge in trade that required more and more merchant shipping. British companies flourished, as did the shipyards that provided them with modern vessels. They carried other countries' trade as well. By the end of the century nearly half the world's merchant tonnage sailed under the British flag.

The image of the sailor changed during the 19th century too. Reforms of entry, training and terms of engagement meant that, from being a casually-employed (or pressed) man who learned, often bitterly, on the job, the naval rating became a trained volunteer in regular service. He often appeared in the papers: 'Jack the Handy Man' always seemed to be part of any British force, resourceful and plucky. Officers too enhanced their status. Now they were prestigious supporters of the state, an emerging empire indeed, and their glittering uniforms and surroundings (for, in spite of coal dust, ships were more and more sparkling as the century went on) added to the glamour surrounding the fleet.

DIRTY BUT DYNAMIC

The world of 19th-century industry: shipyards on the River Clyde, Scotland, 1878.

After the Wars

AGAINST THE PIRATES
HM Proa Jolly Bachelor *(an armed Malay-style craft) beating off an attack by pirates in Borneo, 1843.*

WITH PEACE IN 1815, as always happens after long wars, money and resources for defence declined. The fleet was drastically cut in both ships and manpower. Many professional seamen, both officers and ratings, fell on hard times, while some thanked the lucky stars that had given them prize money. (You will find both sorts in Jane Austen's *Persuasion*.) Some men, like Thomas Cochrane, Earl of Dundonald, sought action in wars of liberation overseas, in South America or the Aegean. Some joined the merchant service. And some were fortunate enough to stay at sea, or in some form of naval employment ashore.

~

There was work to do there. Much of the fleet was worn out after 20 years of war. The most important business of all was thought to be building ships that could withstand a lot of sea service or, alternatively, be laid up in reserve and not rot away while there. The emphasis was on strong construction and durable materials. Overwhelmingly it was still a fleet of wooden sailing ships, although steam as an auxiliary form of power, and iron for construction, were creeping in slowly. Change was rather quicker in the smaller vessels than in the line-of-battle ships. It was these smaller ships, the gunboats and brigs, that saw most action in the first half of the century. The battleships had their day at the reduction of the pirate stronghold at Algiers in 1816, at Navarino in 1827 and at Acre in 1840, all shows of strength in support of stability in the Mediterranean. But in anti-slavery patrols off west and east Africa, in a gigantic charting effort in Africa, the

'I am very much for encouraging this spirit of adventure and I am sure the public feeling is for it.'

John Barrow, Second Secretary of the Admiralty, 1823

J.M.W. Turner's famous picture, The Fighting Temeraire, *movingly captures the maritime evolution of the age, as the wooden-walled veteran of Trafalgar is towed to her final berth by a steam tug.*

A SEARCH IN VAIN

Arctic exploration meant that ships could be trapped in the winter ice, giving their people the unattractive options of sledging out or staying put. The most poignant story was that of Sir John Franklin, who was lost with his crew in 1847 while searching for the Northwest Passage. Lady Franklin, refusing to accept that her husband must have perished, sponsored several fruitless expeditions in search of him. Some remains of the party, with their final messages, were found six years later.

'At Baffin's Bay where the whalefish blows
The fate of Franklin nobody knows.'

Lady Franklin's Lament , 1853

TRAPPED
HMS Hecla *trapped in the ice, 1825. Many Arctic and Antarctic expeditions were undertaken during the 19th century.*

Indian Ocean and the China Seas, and in exploration of the Arctic and Antarctic, it was the small ships that carried out the main naval task.

~

The work, as the logs of these ships and the diaries of their officers show, was arduous, often humdrum and always dangerous. Danger came more from disease than from the violence of the sea or any enemy – though enemies there were, from fighting slavers to Borneo pirates. The losses from fever, though, particularly on the African coasts, were horrendous; one hydrographer of the Navy commented that the charts the surveyors made were coloured with drops of blood.

STEAM AND IRON

STEAM PROPULSION AT SEA ran in close parallel with its use on land. The principle of the engines was the same: water was turned in a boiler to steam, which then provided the energy to push a piston, which turned a crank, which rotated a wheel or shaft. So the railways in the 1820s, and the paddle steamers in the same decade, made their same slow, laboured way.

Improvement came steadily. Stronger materials, more efficient boilers and more sophisticated engines were invented.

Sail, though, was still regarded as the main means of propulsion at sea. Steam was not always reliable, trained engineers were still in short supply, and coal was not always available in the right quantity or quality. Moreover, officers who had been trained in sail were unwilling to accept any other motive power. Consequently, though both warships and merchant vessels were generally fitted with steam engines by the middle of the 19th century, most of them still carried full sailing rigs and often proceeded under sail alone.

Iron, as a material for ship construction, also took some time to become established. The natural aversion to use of a material that clearly was not buoyant was overcome by practical demonstration that air trapped inside a watertight hull enabled an iron craft to float.

However, there were two further problems. First, if the hull was pierced – say by enemy shot – an iron ship would sink where a wooden one might stay afloat. Second, in iron hulls magnetic compasses would

A VISIONARY ENGINEER
I.K. Brunel in 1857 before the mighty chains designed to restrain his enormous vessel SS Great Eastern *on launching. The problems encountered in building the ship hastened his early death.*

behave erratically. Watertight compartments within the hull and scientifically based arrangements for compass correction were the answers, and were introduced. But old prejudices died hard.

Thus, for much of the 19th century, wood was often used to build ships, but increasingly in combination with iron. For example HMS *Warrior*, the first British ironclad warship (1861), had iron frames and an 11-centimetre (4¼-inch) thick iron hull backed by several inches of teak, as well as wooden decks throughout. *Warrior* was Britain's answer to the French *Gloire* which, though in service first, used less iron in construction and was the weaker ship in all aspects.

'France has now commenced to build frigates of great speed but with their sides protected by thick metal plates, and this renders it imperative for this country to do the same without delay.'

Sir Baldwin Walker, Controller of the Navy, 1858

BRITAIN'S FIRST IRONCLAD
HMS Warrior *(1860), now superbly preserved at Portsmouth, was the most powerful warship of her day.*

SCREW VERSUS PADDLE

The principle of the screw propeller had long been known, by Leonardo da Vinci among others. But now steam power led to the idea being revived by Ericsson, Petit Smith and Isambard Kingdom Brunel. The Admiralty was persuaded and, with Brunel's help, built an experimental screw ship, the *Rattler*. After numerous tests and investigations, a series of trials was arranged in 1845 between the *Rattler* and a paddler of similar power, the *Alecto*, culminating in a tug-of-war, the two ships lashed stern to stern, which the *Rattler* won convincingly. The Navy adopted the screw. In the merchant service, Brunel had already introduced it in the *Great Britain*.

ARMOUR AND ARMAMENT

THE OLD FASHION

A gun's crew at drill in 1854. Though gunnery was now systematically taught, little had changed in 200 years.

BREECH LOADING

Early breech-loading guns were unreliable and the Navy reverted to muzzle loaders, but by 1880 better breech-loading designs were in service.

THE FRENCH WERE FIRST to use metal armour for warships. At the assault on Kinburn in the Crimea in 1855, three floating batteries clad in iron formed part of the Anglo-French bombardment force and operated in safety close to the Russian shore artillery; the Russian cannon balls just bounced off, and exploding shells were ineffective.

Other nations took the lesson. Ironclad battleships appeared quickly: the French *Gloire* in four years, the British *Warrior* in six. In America during the Civil War, the southern states improvised iron cladding on existing hulls, while the north, with better manufacturing resources, built low-lying, heavily armoured 'monitors' as well as more conventional ironclads.

In this revolution, many questions confronted the designers. How was armament to be developed that would overcome the new armour? How was it to be arranged in a ship so that it could most effectively be brought to bear? And how were the new arrangements to be reconciled with the means of propulsion, which were still a combination of sail and steam?

A succession of great designers over the next half-century – among those

from Britain Watts, Barnaby, Reed and White, along with many innovative Europeans and Americans – grappled with these problems.

On the way, many of their solutions looked bizarre, but what emerged was the late 19th-century battleship, a potent symbol of maritime power. The main armament remained the big gun which, now rifled for accuracy, threw shell rather than cannon balls, was loaded at the breech rather than the muzzle and used improved propellants and explosives to increase lethality.

All these innovations took time to become established, and the gun did not go unchallenged. Most big ships were fitted with rams, thought to be the surest means of sinking the enemy. Also, both the torpedo and the mine had their passionate advocates. The ram turned out to be an aberration, but the others stayed part of the naval balance in time to come.

Increasingly, guns were fitted in rotating turrets so that they could fire on any bearing. In early installations, efforts were made to combine this with a full sailing rig. However, this soon proved impracticable and, in the case of the ill-designed HMS *Captain* which in 1869 capsized during a storm, fatal. Gradually, in battleships, masts ceased to carry sail and were used only for flag signals. Steam provided the only motive power. However, smaller ships employed far afield, where coal was scarce, combined sail and steam for much longer. But constantly, technical progress was sought in every field of maritime endeavour.

A FATAL COMPROMISE
HMS Captain's *designer tried to combine gun turrets with a full sailing rig. The ship was unstable and she capsized in 1869.*

'Not in vain the distance beacons. Forward, forward let us range, Let the great world spin forever down the ringing grooves of change …'

Alfred, Lord Tennyson, Locksley Hall

JACK SUPPORTS
THE FLAG

*Sailors from a naval brigade
man a Gatling gun at
Alexandria, 1882.*

*'We don't want to fight, but by Jingo, if we do,
We've got the ships, we've got the men, we've got the money too…
And the Russians shall not have Constantino-ple.'*

Music-hall song, 1878

UNTIL THE 19TH CENTURY, the sailor was employed on a casual basis, serving his ship, not the Navy as such. When the ship paid off, his service ceased. In 1830, though, the foundations for a professional Navy career were laid, with standardized training for ratings and regular, renewable engagement and promotion on merit, not seniority. Gunnery training now vied in importance with learning how to handle sail.

The advent of steam brought two new breeds of men. At first the engineers, trained by the manufacturers, came with their machines. Stokers were often ex-miners, muscular men able to withstand an inferno of heat and noise down below. To the seamen both these types were foreign creatures. Even when engineers were incorporated into the Navy, the difference remained.

MIDSHIPMEN'S BERTH

An early 19th-century picture of 'the young gentlemen'. They became more earnest as the century went on.

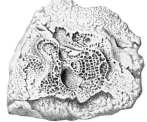

FROM THE DEEP

The voyage of HMS Challenger, 1873–76, carried on the Navy's scientific work, bringing back thousands of specimens from ocean depths.

Shaking down all these increasingly diverse people into a coherent crew was the responsibility of the officers. Their training changed radically too. No longer did young boys enter a ship as 'captain's servant'. Rather, boys in their teens went through an ordered system of training, professional and academic – at first in moored hulks, after 1904 at Dartmouth Naval College. Engineers were trained separately in Plymouth.

Discipline became more humane, with flogging abolished in 1879. Moreover, the exploits of naval brigades in numerous colonial wars brought sailors a new respect from the public. On the world stage too, the British Navy had now become a big player. It seemed that whenever there was an international crisis, Britain had only to threaten action by the fleet and the offending foreign power would back down.

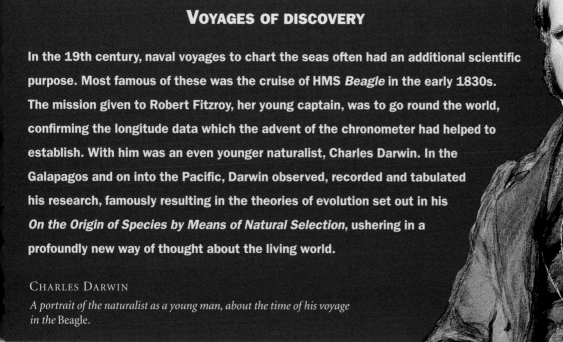

VOYAGES OF DISCOVERY

In the 19th century, naval voyages to chart the seas often had an additional scientific purpose. Most famous of these was the cruise of HMS *Beagle* in the early 1830s. The mission given to Robert Fitzroy, her young captain, was to go round the world, confirming the longitude data which the advent of the chronometer had helped to establish. With him was an even younger naturalist, Charles Darwin. In the Galapagos and on into the Pacific, Darwin observed, recorded and tabulated his research, famously resulting in the theories of evolution set out in his *On the Origin of Species by Means of Natural Selection*, ushering in a profoundly new way of thought about the living world.

CHARLES DARWIN
A portrait of the naturalist as a young man, about the time of his voyage in the Beagle.

POPULAR CUPPA

Demand for tea grew rapidly in the 19th century and supply from India and China was closely linked to maritime trade, and in particular the clipper ships.

UP TO THE MIDDLE OF the 19th century, Britain's economy, and that of of her possessions overseas, was protected by a system of laws, customs duties and taxes, backed by naval forces, which reserved sea traffic and trade very largely for British vessels and financial institutions, a so-called mercantilist system.

But times were changing. Britain was now the 'workshop of the world' and needed to find outlets for her products beyond the old colonies. Free trade arrived; the Navigation Acts which had protected Britain's monopoly in the colonies were repealed, and many of the old customs duties abolished. Soon afterwards, at the end of the war with Russia in the 1850s, the Declaration of Paris put an end to privateering and sought to abolish out-and-out trade warfare.

As a result, the British merchant fleet expanded dramatically, making full use of the home country's industrial capacity. Not only material cargoes were carried; emigrants from England, Scotland and particularly Ireland, as well as many from Europe, travelled to America, Canada, Australia and New Zealand. The increasing British presence in India meant that a new class of administrators and soldiers, with their wives and families, went to the subcontinent.

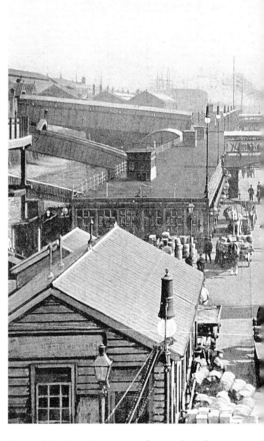

New shipping lines were formed with great energy, many becoming household names: Bibby, British India, P & O, Orient, Blue Funnel and others. Less prestigious were the trampers, picking up cargoes from port to port. Steadily they relied less and less on sail, more and more

'Dirty British coaster with a salt-caked smoke-stack,
Butting through the Channel in the mad March days
With a cargo of Tyne coal, road rails, pig lead,
Firewood, ironware, and cheap tin trays.'

John Masefield, Cargoes

Exceptions to the dominance of steam were the graceful clipper ships that raced their cargoes of tea and wool from the East to home waters. Economic conditions were hard. Clippers needed relatively small crews and could harness the prevailing winds for that particular passage – but around the 1880s they were romantically in the public eye as they strove to bring the first cargoes of the season home. Names such as *Cutty Sark* and *Thermopylae* live on, the *Cutty Sark* being preserved at Greenwich in London, close to the National Maritime Museum.

on steam; the widespread availability of coal supplies – themselves often set in place and replenished by ships – helped this change.

∽

Steadily, too, the needs of the shipping firms were met by construction in British yards. Shipbuilding boomed on the Tyne and the Clyde, where the slipways were constantly busy, though manned by a system of casual labour that was to have grave results a century later. Two facts that today appear almost unbelievable are well supported by the evidence: in 1900, nearly half the world's trade was carried in British ships; and in the same year, over 60 per cent of the world's merchant tonnage was built in British shipyards.

FISHING: A DECLINING HARVEST

FISHING HAS BEEN PART of Britain's maritime scene for hundreds of years. The Romans had a flourishing fish industry and no doubt brought their skills to Britain, while in the Middle Ages the Church insisted on 166 days of fasting in the year, fish being a permitted element. Thus cod and herring became particularly popular.

Until the 16th century, marine fishing was confined to home waters and especially the North Sea, Britain exporting salted herring, salmon and sardine to Europe. Around the same time, herring mysteriously left the Baltic to spawn in the North Sea, spawning also the Scottish fishing industry.

For centuries, the standard fishing boat was the brown-sailed smack, immensely sturdy and manned by seamen whose superb seamanship made up for their coarse ways. A fisherman's life was a hard one, and still is. Crews were small and almost constantly at work, setting and hauling nets, gutting and stowing. Sea conditions were often severe. Pay depended on the size and quality of the catch, generally being a graduated share-out of the proceeds. Many men did make a decent living in return for the marine hazards and domestic anxieties involved.

The Industrial Revolution transformed fishing, making it an important, nation-wide industry. Steam powered both the fishing boats and the trains which moved fish rapidly inland to the cities. Ice-making and refrigeration were also significant innovations, for until then fish had to be preserved by drying, smoking or salting. A large infrastructure quickly built up, with ports such as Aberdeen, Hull, Grimsby, Brixham and Milford Haven supported by transport and

A THOUSAND SHIPS

The herring fleet, Wick, Scotland, in the 19th century.

72

STEAM AND SAIL

A fishing smack (left) and steam drifter, off Great Yarmouth, 1909.

markets both at the coast and inland. By the end of the 19th century, sea fish formed a major part of Britain's diet.

Britain led the way in steam-driven fishing vessels: trawlers towing a net bag along the sea bed for bottom-feeding fish such as cod, haddock and halibut; drifters catching surface feeders such as herring and mackerel in the mesh of a vertically hung net. Steam power and refrigeration meant that trawlers could go farther afield for their catches, anywhere from Morocco to the White Sea. Steam drifters enabled North Sea herring fleets to migrate down the east coast following the fish.

The first major 20th-century development was the diesel engine, which by the 1960s had completely ousted steam power. After the Second World War came sonar, the sending out of sound signals to locate fish shoals. In 1953, in Aberdeen, the world's first factory ship was built, and by the 1960s processing and freezing fish at sea had become commonplace.

At the same time synthetic fibres and improved net design led to greatly increased catches, in turn bringing about the most dramatic change of all; though from the 1880s scientists had challenged theories that the sea's living resources were inexhaustible, by the late 20th century it was clear that the level of fishing in the waters of north-east Europe was unsustainable. Attempts to manage fishery resources under the European Common Fisheries Policy have been highly controversial, and ever stricter quotas have meant a sad and savage reduction of Britain's fishing fleets.

THE MODERN FISHERY

A trawler returning to Kinlochbervie, Scotland, 1994.

SAFETY AT SEA

NORTHERN HEROINE

Grace Darling became nationally famous after rowing with her father to the rescue of a stranded vessel's crew from the rocks of the Farne Islands, Northumberland, 1838.

THE 19TH CENTURY GENERALLY knew of the sea's dangers. Although rescues had been effected ever since Britons first took to the sea, it was only in 1824 that a coordinated service came into being, the result of an appeal to the nation's generosity by Sir William Hillary. In 1854 that service became known as the Royal National Lifeboat Institution (RNLI). Since then lifeboats have changed dramatically, but the work of the RNLI's largely volunteer crews is still supported entirely by donation. The institution's history is illuminated by countless acts of bravery and sacrifice. Since its foundation, over 136,000 lives have been saved.

Less heroic but equally important is the business of keeping ships out of danger in the first place. The Romans established and maintained lights on Britain's shores, though through the Dark Ages the existence of coastal beacons to guide sailors depended largely on the goodwill of monks in isolated outposts.

The venerable company of Trinity House, the body now responsible for safe navigation in British waters, was founded in the 12th century, mainly to prevent the pillage of wrecked ships. After several centuries of free-for-all in coastal safety, from the time of Henry VIII onwards, responsibility devolved gradually upon Trinity House, with a corresponding decline in the company's historically strange and secretive ways. Today Trinity House's main responsibilities are

Salt water – winter	W		
		T	Tropical salt water
Fresh water	F		
		S	Salt water – summer
		W	Salt water – winter
	WNA		Winter in North Atlantic

Before 1876, ships were often overloaded, undermanned or unseaworthy. The Merchant Shipping Act of that year was largely the work of British MP Samuel Plimsoll. It authorized government inspection of ships and made compulsory the painting of a 'Plimsoll' line, to indicate maximum safe levels of loading for salt or fresh water, winter or summer, in tropical and northern waters.

A MODERN LIFEBOAT

These days, besides conventional boats, many RNLI craft are semi-rigid inflatables designed for inshore work.

beaconage (maintaining lighthouses and lightships), buoyage (the placing of buoys to aid navigation) and pilotage (the provision of pilots to guide ships in and out of port). During the 19th century, lights carried by ships, previously seldom fitted at all, were standardized. At the same time the haphazard steering and sailing rules, indicating how ships were to avoid collision when in sight of one another, were codified. These developments all originated in, or were given decisive impetus by, Britain.

Of worldwide importance to shipping is the institution known as Lloyd's of London. This originated in 1688 with

Edward Lloyd, a coffee-house owner who catered particularly for sailors and merchants, reading any news of the sea and ships to them while they took refreshment. In 1770 the marine insurance underwriters and brokers who frequented the place formed an association, calling it Lloyd's. Within a few years they had established a standard insurance policy which has changed little over the years. Today Lloyd's is still an umbrella organization for individuals and syndicates, insuring shipping all over the world against all manner of hazards and eventualities. A separate body, Lloyd's Register of Shipping, was formed in 1834 to monitor the safe construction of merchant ships. The register contains detailed information on any merchant vessel in the world over 100 tons, the expression 'A1 at Lloyd's' becoming the criterion for sound design and workmanship.

TRINITY HOUSE

The coat of arms exemplifies Britain's association with the sea.

GUIDING LIGHT

In spite of today's satellite navigation systems, light-houses are still essential marks for the mariner.

SUPPORTING THE EMPIRE

ALTHOUGH THE WORD 'EMPIRE' had been heard from time to time since the 16th century, until after the Indian Mutiny (1857–58), when the British government assumed responsibility for the subcontinent, there was little sense of an imperial structure in the scattered set of interests, influences, settlements and garrisons that Britain had worldwide, massive in total though these were.

No one gave greater impetus towards formal Empire than Benjamin Disraeli, Conservative Prime Minister during the 1870s. It was he who proclaimed Queen Victoria Queen-Empress of India in 1877, and he who engineered the predominant British interest in the newly opened Suez Canal. He understood too that this maritime Empire, the most sea-based that the world had ever seen, depended for its life on sea communications, and that those communications had in their turn to be backed by reliable sea power.

The means already existed, and were not seriously challenged. The Royal Navy had its battle fleet and its outlying cruisers and gunboats. The merchant navy was the world's largest and most advanced. Bases and coaling stations could be, and were, constructed. Commercial facilities in ports and hinterlands could be developed, backed by diplomacy that was, in turn, backed by demonstrable naval power. It was said that trade followed the flag, but that was

'We wish it to be recognized that, as our Empire has grown by sea power, so by our sea power alone can it be maintained …'

Sir John Knox Laughton, 1891

RULE BRITANNIA!
Her trident symbolized the role which the sea played in Britain's power.

76

too simple an analysis, for just as often the flag followed trade.

Inevitably, there were disasters. In 1852 the troopship *Birkenhead* was lost off the coast of South Africa with the loss of nearly 500 lives. At the mouth of the Peiho in China in 1859, almost as many soldiers and marines died attempting to storm the forts across the mudflats. And many grisly tales emerged from the Indian Mutiny. Yet somehow, even in these reverses, British pluck and resilience seemed to be emphasized. Phrases like 'Women and children first', 'Blood is thicker than water', and even 'Lie back and think of England', entered the language as a direct result.

In consequence, by the late 1870s, some aura of invincibility seemed to surround this maritime empire. Over the next 20 years examples of British dominance were frequent. A Russian foray into Afghanistan was checked by naval manoeuvres in Ireland that were clearly practising a naval assault on the Baltic base of Kronstadt. Turkey was safeguarded through a show of force by the brilliantly handled Mediterranean Fleet passing through the Dardanelles. Rulers disrupting stability in the Middle East were outfaced and finally defeated by

combined naval and military forces in Egypt. It would not last. But for the time, it carried its own salty flavour.

By the turn of the century the three pillars underpinning British dominance – manufacturing power, colonial wealth and maritime supremacy – were eroding at the edges. Rival nations were becoming stronger; new social and political movements threatened the previous order; new technologies, especially in the air and below the sea, presented new problems. Despite all this, the British maritime empire seemed to be at its peak, but a challenge to its dominance was not far away.

COALING SHIP
Bringing coal aboard ship was a frequent operation that involved all hands, not only in stowing the coal but in cleaning up afterwards.

IN FULL POMP
The British Mediterranean Fleet in the 1890s. Its shiny exterior hid considerable fighting efficiency.

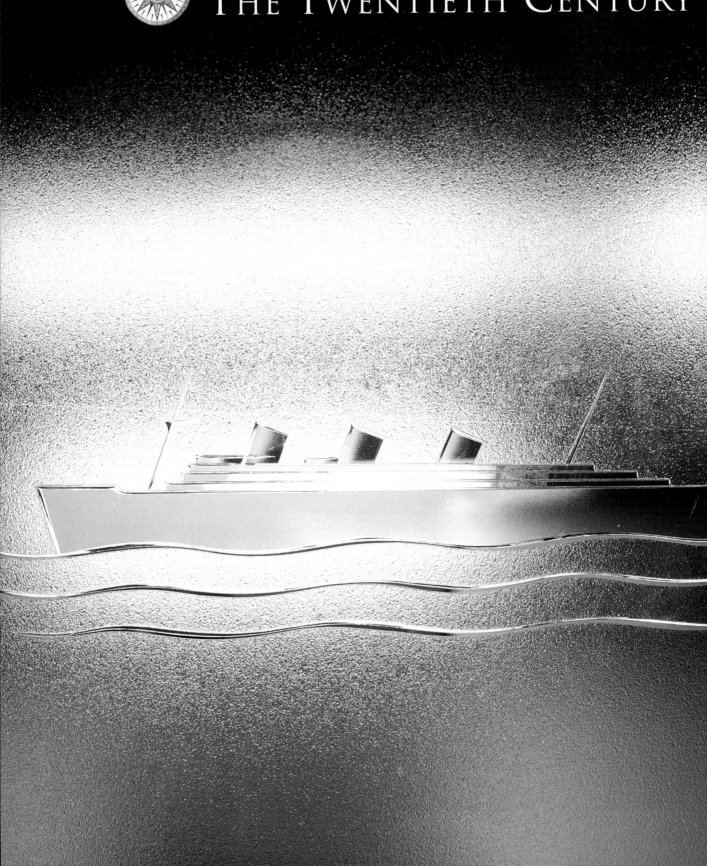

TRANSATLANTIC ART
DECO ELEGANCE
*The image of Cunard's flagship,
RMS* Queen Mary, *etched on a
window on board the liner.*

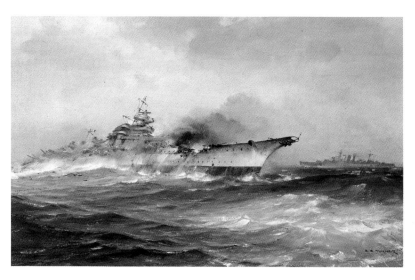

BRITISH MARITIME POWER had peaked in all its aspects, naval, commercial and manufacturing, in the decades before 1914. Given the usual pattern of the growth and decay of nations, decline was inevitable. The process was accelerated by the losses of people and resources in the First World War and the depression of the inter-war years. After the Second World War, which itself involved much further loss, the maritime side of the nation found it particularly hard to recover. It faced a legacy of out-of-date plant, archaic working practices and unimaginative management attitudes. When opportunities did occur, they were generally missed.

Government initiatives to support maritime industry were too little, too late and ineffective. After 1980 they dwindled to nothing. The government's view was that market forces must rule, and they were deaf to arguments that most other nations supported their maritime industries in one way or another. By the end of the century the British merchant marine had declined to a very low level. Shipbuilding was at an even lower ebb, the fisheries were under intense pressure and the Royal Navy's limited resources were overstretched.

The 20th century did have its successes. Royal and merchant navies in both World Wars had been essential factors in victory, and their effectiveness was further demonstrated in the Falklands conflict of 1982. The discovery of North Sea oil and gas and the container revolution in sea transport were challenges that British industry met with some success. The sea was increasingly used for recreation, and the environmental health of the sea and coastline became the subject of lively interest.

Besides this, the Royal Navy and Royal Marines, after the Cold War had ended, saw a wider range of purpose than before, and managed to maintain themselves as an all-arms force with worldwide reach, willing to take part in whatever the new strategic situation might demand.

So at the outset of the new century, with the SeaBritain 2005 initative and signs of renewed support from government, maritime Britain has grounds for confidence.

HUNTER'S END
In May 1941, the German battleship Bismarck, *having sunk HMS* Hood, *itself succumbed after a long chase involving 19 ships.*

PROW OF THE 'MARY'
During fitting out on the Clyde, the great ship shows her elegant lines.

THE FIRST WORLD WAR

*Submarines passing the
Dreadnought, 1910. Wyllie, the
artist, must have understood the
threat one arm posed to the other.*

IN 1913–14 FEW PEOPLE in Britain had any
doubts that war was coming. For
many years Germany and Britain
had vied with each other for
supremacy overseas. Europe bris-
tled with political flashpoints.

In 1897 Kaiser Wilhelm II had
appointed Admiral von Tirpitz
to construct a fleet to challenge
Britain. Tirpitz knew that Germany
could not outbuild the British battle
fleet, but reckoned on threatening
damage to it that Britain, with her worldwide commitments, could not accept,
leaving Germany to acquire the overseas
possessions she desired.

Britain's naval chief, Admiral J.A.'Jacky'
Fisher, countered by introducing
fast battlecruisers and the all-big-
gun *Dreadnought* of 1906. The
Germans were quick to respond,
and by 1914 the two huge fleets –
with up to 30 battleships on either
side – eyed each other across the
North Sea. A naval Armageddon
was awaited. Strategic theory
said that decisive battle would
achieve command of the sea
and subsequent victory.

'JACKY' FISHER
*John Arbuthnot, Lord
Fisher, abrasive and
innovative, dominated
the Royal Navy in the
years before the First
World War.*

Therefore the
larger British
Grand Fleet sought
to bring the German
High Seas Fleet to full
action. German strategy was to
bait the Grand Fleet by raids and sorties,
and, by so doing, catch parts of it with
locally superior force and defeat them. As
to tactics, both battle fleets stuck to the
principle of fighting in a single line so
that all heavy guns could be brought to
bear. More complex formations were
rejected as likely to cause confusion.

On 31 May 1916 German plans misfired
when a sortie of Admiral von Hipper's
battlecruisers, supported by battleships
and intended to isolate and defeat
Admiral Sir David Beatty's battlecruiser
force, resulted in a head-to-head
encounter of both fleets off Jutland.
Everyone, except possibly Hipper, made
mistakes at Jutland. Beatty failed to report
the enemy's position adequately and to
control his supporting fast battleships.
Admiral John Jellicoe, in command of the
Grand Fleet, turned away from a torpedo
attack at a critical moment. Admiral
Reinhard Scheer with his High Seas Fleet
turned back into the jaws of the British
and was lucky to get away with it. The
Royal Navy lost three battlecruisers, two
heavy cruisers and over 5,000 men, far

A U-BOAT DEPARTS
First World War U-boats were small, but nevertheless posed a critical threat.

UNDER FIRE AT JUTLAND

'We were slowly beginning to realize that **all these projectiles falling a few yards short and over were big ones,** and that they were meant for us, and **my thoughts, following their natural course, led me to think of my life-saving waistcoat, which, like a fool, I had left in my sea-chest down below.'**

A midshipman in HMS *Malaya* at the Battle of Jutland

more than at Trafalgar. The Germans lost a battlecruiser and an old battleship. Both sides claimed victory. Strategically, at any rate, the British prevailed for the German fleet made no further serious sortie during the war. It was as well, because a more pressing menace faced maritime Britain. Germany had started the war with a fairly small force of coastal submarines. However, by 1916 this arm was not only stronger but had longer reach. After initial reluctance, the Germans in 1917 decided on unrestricted submarine warfare. This had an immediate effect: although it vastly increased Allied losses, it also brought the USA into the war on the Allied side.

Now it was a race against time, for a starving Britain could yet be knocked out of the war before American power was brought to bear. The situation was saved by the introduction of escorted convoys – a system tried and established over hundreds of years, but at first thought by the professionals to be unworkable in modern conditions. In the meantime, the British maritime blockade in its turn weakened the German economy and will to fight, and the First World War ended with the Allies nominally victorious but, except for the USA, exhausted.

FIRST WORLD WAR ATLANTIC CONVOY
Though introduced late, the convoy system blunted the U-boat menace that vitally threatened shipping in 1916–17.

'It's astounding to me, perfectly astounding, how the very best amongst us absolutely fail to realize the vast impending revolution in naval warfare and naval strategy that the submarine will accomplish!'

Admiral J.A. 'Jacky' Fisher, 1904

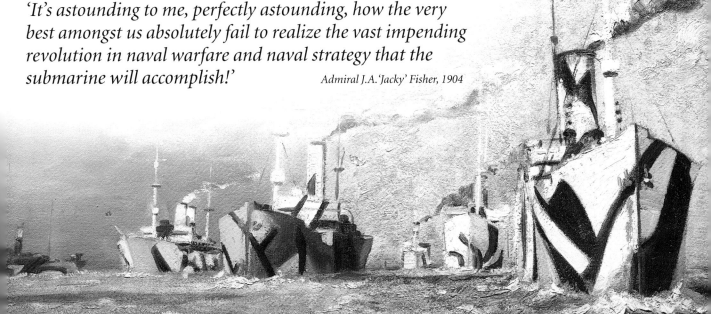

THE GREAT LINERS

TRANSPORTING PEOPLE – as opposed to materials, or mail, or soldiers and their equipment – had been a function of seagoing craft since the beginning of history. St Paul was a passenger when he was shipwrecked off Malta. But it was not until the 19th century that the carriage of civilians became a large-scale industry, and the first few decades of the 20th saw this business reach its peak.

The reasons were various. Firstly, far more people wanted to go overseas. The main motive was economic necessity: the multiplying poor of Europe, including Ireland, saw opportunities that their home countries could not offer and were willing to take the risks of emigration. Also, the expanding empires of European powers demanded large numbers of administrators and merchants to do their work overseas. Secondly, there was no other practicable way to go. Air travel was in its infancy, open only to the rich, and then very often uncomfortable and thought to be hazardous. Finally, the great shipping companies increasingly offered fast, spacious and, for the first-class passenger, luxurious ships that made seagoing in decent weather a pleasure, and encouraged the fashion-able to make frequent voyages.

Competition between the lines – Cunard, White Star, Hamburg-Amerika, Messageries Maritimes, to name only a few – was keen, not only in the levels of accommodation and service which they provided, but also in speed of transit. Nowhere was this more intense than on

FIRST-CLASS LUXURY
The observation lounge of the Queen Mary *shows strong art deco influence.*

DOMINATING THE STREET
The Shaw Savill liner Dominion Monarch *viewed from Saville Street, London, in the 1930s.*

the transatlantic run between the English Channel and New York. The Blue Riband of the Atlantic for the fastest crossing between precisely defined points was hotly contested.

⌇

After the First World War the passenger trade settled into a less frenzied pattern, but the romance of sea travel lived on. Particularly in passages to India and the Far East, shipboard life developed its own mythology. The leisurely pace of the steamers, confinement within their 200 metre (600 feet) or so of regulated space, and the lack of any work to do encouraged flirtations, ridiculous competition in deck games, and often outrageous snobbery as passengers vied for a place at the Captain's Table or other perceived privileges. 'Port out and starboard home', the best (because shadiest) position for cabins on the Red Sea passage, entered the language as the acronym 'posh'.

⌇

The passenger trade, as a commercially viable entity, did not long survive after the Second World War. Air travel grew with great rapidity and aircraft easily supplanted ships with their speed and, eventually, convenience and low cost. Now many ocean liners were without their original purpose, but some found a new one in the cruise business, which boomed as the century came towards its end. Some British companies led in this enterprise, even building new and more palatial ships – but not in British yards.

DREAM TRAVEL

Shipping lines competed fiercely for passengers and freight in the 1920s and 30s, with intense and striking advertising.

THE TITANIC

In 1912 the race for the fastest Atlantic crossing met its nemesis in the sinking of the *Titanic*, the largest and most prestigious of the liners up to that time. On her maiden voyage, seeking to break the record on the northerly (and shortest) route, she struck an iceberg and foundered with great loss of life. Many scandals surrounded this event, not least the lack of adequate lifeboat space.

QUEEN MARY

ATLANTIC RECORD BREAKER

The Queen Mary *made over 1,000 voyages. Within three months of her maiden voyage in May 1936, she had broken six Atlantic speed records and had won the Blue Riband, covering nearly 4,830 kilometres (3,000 miles) in just under four days at an average speed of 30 knots (56kph; 35mph).*

IT WAS SAMUEL CUNARD who first conceived the idea of linking Britain, Canada and the United States by regular passenger and steamship lines. His *Britannia* of 1840 was followed by a succession of transatlantic vessels sporting the famous black and red funnels, each bigger, faster and more splendid than its predecessors.

At 80,000 tonnes and over 300 metres (325 yards) long, the *Queen Mary* represented the zenith of Cunard's dream: the biggest, most luxurious liner of her time, capable of an amazing 30 knots. Yet within four years of her maiden voyage in 1936, this queen of the seas found herself thrust into an alien role vital to the survival of the free, peaceful world she had been built for.

The *Queen Mary* was built in Glasgow and launched in 1934, the work, directly or indirectly, of over 300,000 people. Her very size invited bizarre statistics: three locomotives would fit abreast into any of her funnels; if she were set beside Nelson's Column, the crown of the admiral's hat would just top her boat deck; the 10 million rivets which held her together weighed 4,000 tonnes and would stretch from London to Land's End. Yet, despite her massiveness, her lines, when viewed from the bow, were amazingly graceful. Four steam turbines, supplied by 27 oil-burning boilers, each drove a propeller. With 12 decks and a crew of 1,050, she was designed to carry over 2,000 passengers in five-star luxury surroundings unsurpassed by any predecessor.

However, not long after the Second World War broke out, the *Queen Mary* suffered the indignity of being stripped of her luxurious trappings. As a troopship in battleship grey, with sister ship *Queen Elizabeth*, she spent five years zig-zagging back and forth across the Atlantic, too fast for any U-boat – this despite Hitler's offer of a fortune in cash and the Iron Cross to any commander who could sink her. So it was that in the summer of 1942 the *Queen Mary* came to race from New York to Scotland carrying a staggering 16,000 troops – a complete US division – more passengers than any ship before or since. Men even slept five bunks deep in her swimming pool!

After the war the *Queen Mary* returned to the role of luxury liner on the transatlantic run, being retired in 1967 to become a floating hotel in Long Beach, California. Even now, her size and beauty make her an object of awe, even veneration.

DUNKIRK, 1940
Over 300,000 British and Allied soldiers were evacuated to continue the war. Naval, merchant and recreational craft all helped.

'The only thing that ever really frightened me during the war was the U-boat peril.'
Winston Churchill,
The Second World War

BETWEEN THE WARS, the Royal Navy thought hard about many things: how to get Jutland right if an action like that should happen again; how to use aircraft; how to defend against submarines. The offensive spirit and initiative were emphasized; they trained well. When it came, the Second World War was a more maritime affair than the First, and far beyond the imaginings of the inter-war years. It was a truly global struggle. There never had been, and very probably never will be again, a maritime war on the same scale.

The Atlantic was the most critical theatre. Britain depended entirely on supplies across this ocean, contested by U-boats waging an unrestricted campaign from the first days. The convoy system was implemented straight away, but with meagre sea and air support. Soon the

Germans controlled the whole coastline of continental Europe. The so-called Battle of the Atlantic swayed this way and that, with terrible losses to merchant vessels and warships until, in the first months of 1943, a combination of new ships, aircraft and means of detection gave the Allies the upper hand. Then it was the turn of the U-boats to suffer huge relative casualties, 70 per cent of them being sunk over the whole war.

The German surface force was outnumbered but powerful. The pocket battleship *Graf Spee* was destroyed in the River Plate (1939) and the mighty *Bismarck*, after she had herself sunk the Navy's HMS *Hood*, in 1941. The equally powerful *Tirpitz* was a concern for years, based as she was in northern Norway, close to the route for the vital convoys to Russia. She was eventually sunk by RAF bombing. The *Scharnhorst* died fighting one winter night off the North Cape.

Meanwhile, in the Mediterranean the Fleet was hard pressed. After early success at Cape Matapan and the brilliant Fleet Air Arm attack on Taranto, enemy land-based aircraft inflicted heavy losses off Crete and on the convoys that resupplied Malta. Operation Pedestal, the most vital of these, lost two-thirds of the merchant ships involved, but Malta survived.

In the Far East, the loss of the battleships *Prince of Wales* and *Repulse* in 1941 – again to land-based aircraft – was the

THE VOYAGE OF THE HOPEMOUNT

In 1942, the British tanker *Hopemount* spent nearly 10 months in the icy and stormy waters north of Russia, supplying Russian and British ships with fuel. She sailed almost as far as the Pacific and back again, suffering damage and privation, a feat exceptional even by the standards of the merchant navy.

worst reverse, but by the end of the war the Royal Navy contributed a sizeable Pacific Fleet to supplement the huge American involvement.

This came, though, after the most spectacular maritime effort of the war, the massive 'Operation Overlord' to invade Europe through the Normandy beaches on D-Day, 6 June 1944. The sea side of 'Overlord' was about 70 per cent British, carefully planned by Admiral Ramsay,

mastermind of the Dunkirk evacuation in 1940, and precisely executed.

The merchant and Royal navies, and the Women's Royal Naval Service, came out of the Second World War with huge credit. Their losses were great – 30,000 merchant seamen alone – but they had demonstrated the utmost capacity to absorb change and expansion, great resilience and above all that characteristic of the British at sea: tenacity.

A GLOBAL CONFLICT

More than the First, the Second World War was a global, maritime struggle. In this dramatic painting, an Arctic convoy takes supplies to Russia.

D-DAY, 1944

Troops disembarking from landing craft under fire. Britain provided 70 per cent of the maritime effort.

WINGS AT SEA

SEA WARFARE WAS TRANSFORMED in the 20th century, extending now into the depths below and into the air above. It was still a struggle for control of the surface, because that was where supplies and people passed. Submarines menaced that control, and have their place elsewhere in this book. It was the air element, however, that was in many ways even more pervasive.

Ten years after the first powered flight in 1903, the Royal Navy was experimenting with the launch of aircraft from ships, and by the end of the First World War was operating several vessels that were recognizably aircraft carriers, conducting air raids across the North Sea.

Between the two world wars, however, the momentum for change was lost. The big gun was still thought to be the decisive weapon, with aircraft useful mainly in a reconnaissance role. Moreover, the formation of the Royal Air Force meant difficulties in organizing the flight departments of ships and a low priority in the provision of suitable aircraft. This applied not only to ship-borne machines,

EARLY DAYS
HMS Furious, *a heavy cruiser, was converted as an aircraft carrier in 1918 and again, more fully, in the 1920s.*

THE 'STRINGBAG'
The derogatory nickname for the Fairey Swordfish torpedo bomber did not prevent its stunning success at Taranto in 1940.

SKI JUMP TAKE-OFF
A Harrier jump-jet leaves HMS Hermes *for combat air patrol off the Falklands, May 1982.*

but to the shore-based maritime patrol aircraft that were to prove so essential in the Atlantic campaign.

So at the outset of the Second World War in 1939 the Royal Navy still had much to learn about the potential of maritime air power. The attack on Taranto in 1940 was the first proof of what its ship-borne aircraft could do, and later the Fleet Air Arm critically damaged the *Bismarck*. The importance of the air against submarine threats was eventually recognized; in 1943 long range RAF maritime patrol aircraft came into the Atlantic campaign, and small aircraft carriers supported the convoys.

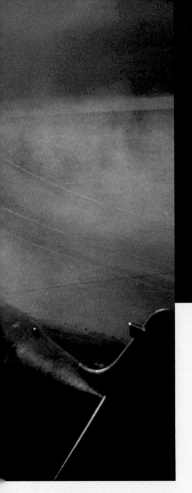

LANDING ON A CARRIER

Landing a fast aircraft on a carrier's small flight deck is a precise and hazardous operation. Before the invention of the mirror landing sight to tell an aircraft whether it was on the right flight-path, it was guided in by signals from a skilled 'batsman'.

'I thought I was coming in low enough, but I was fifty feet up when the batsman gave "cut"; And loud in my earholes the sweet angels sang Float float float float float float float float float PRANG!'

The Fleet Air Arm 'A25' song; Form A25 is a pilot's accident report

At the end of the war the British Pacific Fleet operated alongside the US Navy in carrier warfare. Sturdy as the British carriers proved against Japanese kamikaze attacks, they were unable to mount anything like the volume of air effort of their US counterparts and their supply arrangements were cumbersome.

In the post-war decades, the Fleet Air Arm struggled hard against continually diminishing resources. This did not stop the inventive British bringing in some important 'firsts': the angled deck to avoid deck-park accidents, the mirror sight to aid deck landings, and the steam catapult to give extra boost on take-off.

But in 1966 government decreed that there were to be no more big aircraft carriers. The naval planners manoeuvred round this by pursuing a 'through-deck cruiser' design that eventually became the 'Invincible' class, capable of operating Sea Harrier jump-jets. The Falklands campaign of 1982 proved their worth. Helicopters had a variety of roles – anti-submarine, troop-carrying, early warning, rescue and transfer – and operated from all major ships including the Royal Fleet Auxiliary. At the same time, the Royal Air Force developed its highly capable Nimrod long-range anti-submarine aircraft. Maritime aviation struggled, but would not give up.

WHAT'S IN A NAME?
Initially called 'through-deck cruisers' for political reasons, the 'Invincible' class were eventually admitted by the Navy to be aircraft carriers.

The Navy since 1945

'Our vital interests are not confined to Europe ... the focus for our maritime forces ... will move towards rapid deployment operations.'

UK Strategic Defence Review, 1998

DETERRENT PATROL

HMS Victorious, *nuclear-powered and armed with Trident ballistic missiles, sets out to maintain the UK's nuclear deterrent.*

DESTROYER

Type 42 destroyers were an essential element of fleet air defence in the 1980s and 1990s.

BRITAIN HAD OVER 800,000 naval personnel at the end of the Second World War. The majority of these were fairly soon 'demobbed', but the Navy still had a lot of men and ships. In consequence, they found it hard to come to terms with the circumstances of the 1950s and 1960s. Money was scarce, yet at the same time the technical options were tantalizingly diverse. Nuclear weapons were a reality, nuclear power for submarine propulsion was feasible, carrier aviation was making rapid progress, and advances in electronics meant better detection of opponents, communication with friends, and guidance for missiles.

The perceived need to keep up in all of these departments was sharpened by the emergence of a new potential enemy in the shape of the Soviet Union. The North Atlantic Treaty Organization (NATO) was formed to counter this real threat, and the Soviet Navy was developed by its great Commander-in-Chief Admiral Gorshkov into a potent force that could confront even the mighty United States Navy. Royal Navy planners made much of the need to match the Soviet Navy, if not in numbers at least in capability.

But the Navy's other tasks were seen by the politicians as dwindling. The Suez campaign in 1956 had been a military success but a political failure, and each of the numerous quasi-wars of the 1960s was thought to be a one-off, post-colonial affair. So, in 1966, it was announced that no new fixed-wing aircraft carriers were

THE FALKLANDS FACTOR

In the early 1980s the Royal Navy's hard-won equilibrium was threatened by stringent cuts in the latest government defence review. Air and amphibious capacity was particularly at risk. But very soon after the measures were announced, Argentina invaded the Falkland Islands and Britain embarked on a hazardous but successful effort to recover them. At 13,000 kilometres (8,000 miles) from the UK, it was an overwhelmingly maritime enterprise, and the Navy was saved thereafter from the more extreme of the planned reductions.

to be built, and in early 1968 that in future the only justification for maritime forces would be NATO missions – the NATO area extending only to the Mediterranean and North Atlantic.

The Navy clawed its way back. It was already commissioning nuclear-powered submarines, including ballistic missile boats to carry the nuclear deterrent, and carried through its plans for 'through-deck cruisers', which were eventually admitted to be small aircraft carriers. Just as importantly, it preserved a Royal Fleet Auxiliary that could supply it at sea all round the globe, and it persuaded the Foreign Office to support it in mounting worldwide deployments by relatively large groups of combatant ships.

The rapid break-up of the Soviet Union around 1990 took most by surprise. Governments took some time to adjust to the situation, but by the mid 1990s a pattern of fighting services was emerging that stressed flexibility and adaptability in the face of this new, turbulent world. The crews of ships changed too: women now were part of most surface ships' companies, and the WRNS was absorbed into the Royal Navy. Whatever the future might bring, it was accepted that maritime power would often have a critical role to play.

ROYAL YACHT BRITANNIA
Launched in 1953, HM Queen Elizabeth II's coronation year, Britannia *completed 968 royal voyages before being decommissioned in 1997. Now permanently moored at Leith, she is Edinburgh's leading tourist attraction and corporate events venue.*

THE SEA BUSINESS SINCE 1945

CONTAINER TRADE

P & O Nedlloyd's Remuera *at night. Though British/Dutch owned, she sails under the Liberian flag.*

BRITAIN ENDED THE SECOND World War with a large but badly worn merchant navy. By contrast, the USA had a vast, new, hurriedly-built merchant fleet – although many ships were soon transferred to other flags or put into reserve. Most other countries had seen their fleets reduce in number.

Thus when trade inevitably expanded after the war, there were tremendous opportunities for any country which was willing to seize them. Britain missed out. Oil tankers were not built fast enough

and ships for ore, grain and other bulk cargoes were equally slow to leave the slipways. And when containers were introduced from the 1960s onwards, again Britain lagged behind.

There were several reasons for this. Labour relations and regulations, at sea and in the ports, were cumbersome and costly. Management was timid, having suffered burnt fingers in the inter-war years; post-war booms and slumps made them more so. International competition was fierce, both in economic and political terms.

Decline accelerated in the 1980s, with shipowners burdened by more tax, not less. So, by the mid 90s only a few hundred ocean-going merchant ships flew Britain's red ensign. Complete extinction became a possibility. There were some hopeful signs: for example, British owner-ship of ships sailing under other flags remained quite strong. But ships that flew the famous 'red duster' were a surer asset, and in 2001 the government introduced the tonnage tax which boosted the return of British ships to their proper flag.

The great yards that 100 years before had built over half the world's ships declined even faster than the fleets they served. Archaic working practices and plant, together with uncertain demand, and competition from Far Eastern yards all contributed to a situation where now the home industry is scarcely capable of producing, from wholly British sources, a large state-of-the-art ship. Even warships, so long the mainstay of some yards, are now often assembled from components manufactured separately, and not all in the United Kingdom.

Fisheries also tell a sad tale. The European Common Fisheries Policy, imposed upon Britain as the price for entry into the Common Market in 1973 has, on the whole, harmed the British fishing indus-try. Stock depletion, over-fishing, quotas, negotiations and dubious practices all played a part.

Yet, hearteningly, the maritime sector still accounts for five per cent of Britain's Gross Domestic Product. Some of this comes from services provided by City of London institutions: brokerage, insur-ance, law and safety classification. More comes from hi-tech developments in

NORTH SEA OIL

A booming marine resource in the 1980s and 90s, North Sea oil and gas continue to supply the nation.

charting, instrumentation, exploration and harnessing of the sea's resources.

A further bright spot is the use of the sea for recreation, which grows year by year. Sailing and power boats, diving, and all forms of water sport are popular as never before, supported by innovative and flour-ishing construction and manufacturing. All these are positive signs that the sea has still much to offer in the life of the nation.

FERRY WORK

In spite of competition from the Channel Tunnel, many ferries cross daily between Britain, France and Belgium.

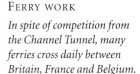

INTO THE TWENTY-FIRST CENTURY

'Freedom and Western values have not arrived by chance, but are rewards for our maritime past.'

Peter Padfield, historian and winner of the Mountbatten Prize for Maritime Literature, 2003

TWENTY-FIRST-CENTURY SEA HEROINE
Ellen MacArthur, the youngest Briton to circumnavigate the world single-handed and the fastest woman ever to do so.

THE 200TH ANNIVERSARY OF the Battle of Trafalgar in 2005 is a highly appropriate moment to celebrate Maritime Britain – drawing inspiration from the glories of yesterday and also planning new opportunities for tomorrow. SeaBritain 2005 celebrates Britain's maritime heritage and its future, through new initiatives in publicity, training and technology such as SeaVision and VisitBritain. In the 21st century, the British still look seawards, enjoy the varied coastal landscapes of their islands, and flock to see ships – as is evident by the success of several International Festivals of the Sea, with tall ships from many nations on view alongside the latest naval vessels.

The sea shaped the spirit of enterprise and adventure that gave Britain much of its national character. As this book has

sought to show, Britain's history has been intimately bound up with the sea and ships. While no longer 'master and commander' of the world's oceans, Britain remains uniquely positioned to benefit from the sea: in trade and merchant shipping; the prudent use of marine resources; the use of naval power for good; international safety at sea; and in education, recreation and heritage. Such is the widest, yet most satisfying, definition of 'sea power': the ability to use the sea. Britain may no longer rule a maritime empire, but it can surely make the most of the assets left to us by history, geography and generations of seafarers.

QUEEN MARY 2
The huge transatlantic liner commissioned in 2004, French-built but flying the British flag.

INDEX